GAMBLING LIFE

THOMAS M. MALABY

Gambling Life

Dealing in Contingency

in a Greek City

UNIVERSITY OF ILLINOIS PRESS

URBANA AND CHICAGO

Library of Congress Cataloging-in-Publication Data
Malaby, Thomas M., 1967–
Gambling life : dealing in contingency in a Greek city /
Thomas M. Malaby.
p. cm.
Includes bibliographical references and index.
ISBN 0-252-02828-7 (cloth : alk. paper)
1. Gambling—Greece—Chania. 2. Social interaction—
Greece—Chania. 3. Chania (Greece)—Social life
and customs. I. Title.
GN454.6.M35   2003
306.4'2—dc21   2002014271

For Cristina and Julian

[They] were apt to pay attention to signs and portents other men had no inkling of. For them the web of cause and effect was invisible and simultaneously everywhere, which was why a man could sink his net with salmon one night and catch only kelp the next. Tides, currents, and winds were one thing, the force of luck another.

—David Guterson, *Snow Falling on Cedars*

The plate of the hunter, the gambler, and the fisherman is nine times empty and one time full.

—Cretan proverb

Contents

Preface

This book is a product of an ongoing attempt to answer a question that has repeatedly caught my attention since I began studying anthropology: How do people come to understand the "distribution of fortunes" in the world (Weber 1946, 275)? Weber's own pursuit of an answer to this question has left a lasting legacy in social science, but within this legacy this question has too often been reduced to that of theodicy, that is, the moral paradox posed by the existence of suffering under a religious framework that presupposes a benevolent and omnipotent god. I assert, however, that there is a deeper sociological aspect of the question contained in Weber's project, one that is prior to its particular realization in the issue of theodicy. This aspect is that of indeterminacy itself as a feature of human experience. Framed in this way, the issue of indeterminacy generates two kinds of sociological investigations, what might be called objectivist and interpretive, and my goals in this book reflect this dual agenda. One on hand, I seek to sketch out a new language for identifying and discussing indeterminacy from an analytical point of view. In this sense, this project is in some sense a constructive one—an attempt to escape the straitjacket of risk and fate that academics have inherited and that is desperately unexamined and antiquated. On the other, I seek to draw attention to how unexpected outcomes are interpreted and accounted for by individuals, groups, and institutions to establish or maintain moral and political legitimacy. These two objectives at times lie uneasily alongside one another, but I believe this juxtaposition is a productive one. To focus on meaning and power alone would be as reductive as it would be solely to explore how we can chart indeterminacy as a universal aspect of human experience.

Choosing to study the social processes surrounding gambling events to reach these goals is in one sense a natural move given the longstanding reliance on metaphors of game playing in theories of social action. But in doing so I am also working through, as it happens, my own lifelong fascination with games, which began in a household that relied on them as a forum for sociality and grievance. In this sense, the city of Chania in Greece was almost immediately a familiar territory because of the similar prominence of games in everyday Greek life. However, to pursue the questions raised by the issue of indeterminacy demands that I incorporate this examination of the domain of gambling into other arenas of experience where chance also resides, and therefore this book, though organized by its focus on gambling, is as much an attempt to gain insight into the uncertain realms of tourist entrepreneurship, courtship and kinship, criminality, and mortality as it is an ethnography of gambling practice. Throughout this book, then, I am pursuing an understanding of the meaningful connections that Greeks in Chania make across these domains but also seeking to identify the various sources of unpredictability that predominate across and among them.

In pursuing and completing this project I have relied on the good will and good advice of many people and the support of generous institutions. I would like first to thank the gamblers and other residents of Chania who welcomed my intrusive questions and patiently taught me not simply the rules of the many games they played but also how to play and understand them. Although I have used pseudonyms throughout this book to protect their privacy, I would like to note my appreciation to several here using their real names. In particular I thank and remember Vangelis Vranas, a good friend who did not live to see this work completed. Other Chaniots who deserve special mention for their assistance and friendship include Elpidha Katsantoni and Rudi Riegler, Sophia Liggouri, Lori Little, Noriko Komine, and Khristoforos Sklavonitis. In addition I wish to extend my gratitude to the staff and faculty of the Ithaca Program—at the time of my research situated in Chania—including Nikos and Ann Yermanakos and Joan Neumann for their warm hospitality. I am deeply indebted to Noufris Papatzanakis and Lotte Neumann for their guidance, friendship, and hospitality; many of the ideas in this work had their genesis in long and engaging conversations in our favorite places in Chania.

The research on which this work is based was most intensively carried out in two visits over a period of eighteen months from September

1994 through February 1996. It was supported by a Fulbright-Hays Fellowship for Doctoral Dissertation Research Abroad and a Krupp Foundation Dissertation Research Fellowship through the Minda de Gunzberg Center for European Studies at Harvard University. Chip Ammerman and George Dariotis of the Fulbright office in Athens provided invaluable assistance and hospitality. Subsequent visits of shorter duration, one supported by a Faculty Travel Award from the University of Wisconsin at Milwaukee, have supplemented these findings. Time to complete final preparation of the manuscript was generously made available by the University of Wisconsin at Milwaukee, and I thank in particular J. Patrick Gray, chair of the Department of Anthropology, and Eleanor Miller, associate dean for the social sciences.

Fellow students in the anthropology department of Harvard University provided intellectual stimulation and camaraderie as they patiently read and discussed much of this work, especially Bartholomew Ryan, Josh Breslau, Levent Soysal, Andreas Glaeser, Komatra Chuengsatiansup, Don Seeman, Ann Frechette, Matthew Kohrman, Melissa Caldwell, and Brian Palmer. I am enormously grateful for all of their input. Many other friends, colleagues, and teachers have graciously read and commented on parts of this work, including Daphne Berdahl, David Sutton, Fredrik Barth, Vangelis Calotychos, Terry Roopnaraine, André Levy, and Christina vonMayrhauser. Arthur Kleinman and Stanley Tambiah provided invaluable guidance through their careful attention to this project and their insightful comments. Peter Klibanoff and Andrew Guzman have been treasured resources for economic treatments of uncertainty—above and beyond the call of duty for such close friends. Ingrid Jordt and Kalman Applbaum at the University of Wisconsin at Milwaukee have provided both sustenance and substantive insight in many tea-laden conversations as this book reached its final stages. Paul Brodwin, Cheryl Ajirotutu, and Bill Washabaugh have also helped make UWM a welcoming and exciting place for me to carry out this work. Of course, whatever shortcomings remain in this text are wholly my own.

I owe the deepest debt of gratitude to Michael Herzfeld. His unflagging support and keen insight inspired me through all phases of this endeavor, and his untiring willingness to introduce me to anthropology and Cretan life is a testament to his generous spirit.

At the University of Illinois Press, Joan Catapano and Theresa L. Sears have been wonderfully supportive and diligent. It has been a pleasure working with them. My thanks also to Janet Hart for her many helpful and detailed comments, as well as her suggestion of a title.

I also wish to thank my parents, David and Loretta Malaby, and my brothers, Steve and Mark Malaby; they have long been and continue to be my guides on a long journey, even through the dark.

Last and most important of all, this work simply would not have been completed without the support of my wife, Cristina Hernandez-Malaby. This book is dedicated to her and to our wonderful son, Julian, who has brightened many a long and otherwise text-filled day.

GAMBLING LIFE

Introduction:
Engaging Uncertainties

Veiled Practices and Hidden Portals

It was New Year's Eve, 1995, and I was watching the aftermath of a poker game at a small *kafenio* (coffeehouse) in Chania, Crete. It had been quiet there all evening, with only one continuous game of poker, and the owner was standing and railing against the lack of business. Nondas had purchased the *kafenio* from Petros, a friend of mine, the previous spring, and this was his first holiday season as owner.[1] The previous New Year's Eve under Petros's ownership the place had been nearly full (in fact, it had been full that entire week), with about ten or twelve dice gamblers and about seven or eight others. Petros was there this evening, having just played with Nondas and two others while another customer and I looked on. Petros and a player I knew only slightly had had good nights, and everyone was cashing out (exchanging markers for money), each player counting his unruly pile of the small, old cards (*khartakia*) that they used as markers into neat stacks of twenty.[2] Not only was Nondas having a bad evening as the owner, but he had not had a good night at cards either, and during the cashing out he paid the other player who had been winning about 60,000 Dr (about US$250) and then paid Petros about 38,000 Dr (about US$160). "I'll pay you later," he had said to Petros, alluding to the balance of about 20,000 Dr that he still owed. "No problem," replied Petros easily, not even glancing up.

Now Nondas was letting everyone know that he had gone to the expense of having a dicing surface made for *zaria,* the dice game popular at this time of year, a rectangular one large enough to be laid across two poker tables. With a low (about two-inch-high) rail encircling it and a broad expanse of green baize, it looked a bit exposed with no one standing around it, and it was strikingly visible from the street because of the large amount of green it presented. There was no fear of police, however, because of all nights in Greece New Year's Eve is the one when all Greeks, from children to adults, men and women, are expected to gamble "for the good of the [coming] year" (*"yia to kalo tou khronou"*). The law against gambling, though still in effect, is not enforced on this night. Nondas gestured expansively at the lonely table, cursing it and his own luck: "I screw my misfortune!" (*"Gamo tin atikhia mou!"*), "What else could I have done? And the bastards don't even stop by to play for a little while! And what am I going to do with this?" Waving a hand at the dice surface, he asked, "You know how much this cost?"

Before long Petros turned to me and said, "Let's go." We walked in the cool night air along the darkened side street in the newer part of town; the street rose ever so slightly as we walked south, away from the ocean, where behind us nestled the old harbor of Chania. We were about five blocks south of the main thoroughfare of the city when Petros stopped; in this area the large (five- to six-story) apartment and office buildings began to give way to individual homes. Petros turned to go into a card-playing coffeehouse that I had not entered before. The *kafenio* was small, crowded, and noisy. Because it was on the corner of a modernist, postwar-era, multistory building (and the street), large plate glass windows filled two of its sides. A few small tables were near the entrance, with the small bar directly across from the door. To the left, along the windows, were two large card tables, one of which was being used. Here the familiar smell of cigarettes, coffee, and sweat that only a large crowd in a small room creates hung in the air. About twenty-five people were in the room, and I wondered what could account for the crowd because only one table was being used, and that one for blackjack, a comparatively low-stakes game. Two young women busily filled orders behind the bar. We sat down for just a moment and ordered drinks. The owner, Mikhalis, appeared, smiling at Petros and coming over to say hello to him. We met, and shortly thereafter I was surprised and intrigued to see a hitherto nondescript wood panel along the left-hand wall slide to the left; I began to hear the sounds of *zaria* being played—the calling of bets and tumbling of dice. I was ushered into the side room, one wall of which was, like the front room, made up of a large window to the street. A heavy, light-blocking curtain had been hung across it, however, with the inside edges pinned together in several places to ensure that little light would escape to the street.

In this room, there were two tables for dicing: one in front, next to the window, and the other behind. The front table was very crowded, with about twenty players sitting around it (all back a fair distance from the table surface to accommodate the crowd); there were about eight players at the back one. The players were between about forty and sixty years old, although there were a few younger players, especially at the back table. The back table was for lower-stakes *zaria* (anywhere from 3,000 Dr to 60,000 Dr on each bet [about US$12–240], with the most common bet about 10,000–15,000 Dr [about US$40–60]), and the other was for higher stakes (each bet ranging from 10,000 to 120,000 Dr, with the most common being about 40,000 Dr [US$40–480 range, about US$160 the most common]). Circular fluorescent lights hung above each table, and they gave the room a slight blue- and gray-tinged ambiance.

These tables for *zaria* were special, at first glance similar to most of the poker tables I had seen in town but in fact very different. They were about the same size as the poker tables, and like them had circular surfaces covered with green baize, but they also were edged—like Nondas's newly made but unused one—by a circle of wood that created a small wall surrounding the playing surface; this kept the dice on the table and provided a surface for the players to place bets. Underneath the table was another surface, halfway to the floor, also circular—another table, in effect—that was slightly larger than the upper surface and provided space for drinks, cigarettes, lighters, and ashtrays. One effect of this design was that the players could not sit close to the table—the lower shelf took away any space for one's legs—and therefore a large number of chairs could fit around it, creating an open situation (in sharp contrast to the closed, four-person poker game as it is played in Chania, where each player fairly perches over one quarter of the table, elbows and chips further spreading across and defining the space). Here, as they played *zaria*, the players sat back from the table, leaning forward to place bets and take and toss the dice.

Seats and a small table were brought in and placed along a side wall, and there we sat and watched the dicing for a while. We sipped our coffee as some of the players called out, offering bets on one of the two players dicing against each other, spreading their arms, imploring, "*Ela tora! Dheka egho!*" ("Come now! Ten thousand on the player with the dice!"). Others instead nearly chanted, in near-monotone voices, while sitting still and scanning the table with their eyes: "*Ena taliro esi, ena taliro esi*"

("Five thousand on the other player, five thousand on the other player"). *"Egho"* ("I") and *"Esi"* ("You") indicate, in the context of *zaria*, the current roller of the dice and the other player, respectively.[3] Other players sat nearly still, watching the dice and table continuously, turning their heads only briefly to take bets with a nod or word. With a rhythmic regularity, dice bounced and clattered across the tables, the sounds alternating with the sharp clacking of the dice as they were shaken in the throwers' hands. All players threw in a deliberate manner, but there were a number of distinct styles. Some flipped the dice upward as they dropped their hands quickly below the edge of the table; others lofted the dice high into the air, at times nearly striking the suspended lamps above.

Before long a small, older man at the front (high-stakes) table, dressed in a neat, pale green linen suit, leaned back and called one of the women serving drinks over to him. He whispered something in her ear, and she went back to the outer room. She returned in a moment and I watched as she discreetly passed a sizable wad of 5,000-Dr bills to him. Petros was also watching, and in response to my questioning glance he leaned over to me and whispered, "He has a large bag of money behind the bar, with, maybe, 2 or 3 million drachmas." The transaction was remarkable for its apparent discretion, which nonetheless clearly failed amidst the roving eyes of the room; it was obvious that we were not the only ones who had noticed it, even though the other players had only briefly glanced his way. But this of course raised a further question: As the man was more than plausibly aware of being seen, why had he even bothered to attempt to hide it? Performances on performances, games on games—the evening's strategizing did not reside solely at the poker table.

Later Petros decided to play some blackjack in the front room, and I watched as he played in a group of about eleven. Throughout the evening, as I entered either of the rooms after a significant absence, most of the players and other customers looked at me carefully. This was not a new experience for me; almost all fair-complexioned, short-haired, English (native) speakers around in the wintertime in Chania are Americans from the nearby NATO naval base at Soudha Bay, which has a large U.S. contingent. It was no different when I sat down near the blackjack table, which I had not approached during my brief time in the outer room just after I had arrived. One player, sitting quite near me, regarded me for a few minutes before saying forcefully, in English, "Do you want to play?" It was obvious to me and the others that, apart from the invitation itself, behind his words were the following questions: "Do we fascinate you so much? Why is this place of interest to you?" By inviting me into the activity, he ironically called attention to my outsider status—a local would have needed no invitation to join in—and the use of English further underscored this distinction. I answered in Greek, "Not now, thanks, maybe later," and his expression changed to surprise, as did that of others around the table following the conversation. A man sitting next to him started chuckling while he turned to the first man and said, "He speaks Greek!" and slapped him on the shoulder. As I continued to sit nearby, the man who spoke English began to engage me in conversation, this time in Greek, asking where I was from in the United States. It turns out that Yorgos had lived in Seattle for twenty years. Later on, another player across the table asked the waitress, loud enough for all of us to hear, to get a drink "for the American," meaning not me but the man who had originally challenged me.[4] An encounter across nationalities had quickly become fodder for the jibes of local competitiveness.

As I walked home the sky began to lighten with the coming morning, and the experiences of the evening—the crossing of boundaries of secrecy, sociability, and nationality—prompted a memory of a similar walk I had taken many months before, at dusk on a day shortly after my arrival in Chania in the fall of 1994. Eager to begin to learn where the gambling in Chania took place, I had walked first along the broad avenues that cut through the urban landscape, avenues that connect the major squares in the newer part of the city: one in front of the courthouse, another in front of the central market, a third near the high school and soccer stadium. I soon discovered that it was not necessary to move into the back alleyways and small streets to find coffeehouses where card playing was the main attraction; from the main boulevards I began to catch glimpses (and learn how to do so) of green baize and hanging lamps, of circles of seated players with perhaps an onlooker or two. But each of these places, as prominently situated as they were, challenged the passersby to view anything but this barest glimpse. One location, on a broad residential avenue heading from the courthouse to the sea, had a deep, roofed patio, with the back wall lined with potted plants that grew to obscure almost completely the paned windows. Another place, near the courthouse itself, had large windows across the front, but I saw first only a sitting area with a television, and behind this a low rail with small tables behind it. Only then did the edges of a few circular card tables catch my eye, but by then a wall had interceded: The coffeehouse was *L*-shaped, with the card tables grouped around the corner. The card playing in Chania seemed paradoxically conspicuous yet nearly unseen, and as I finally arrived at home as the sun rose on New Year's Day months later, I felt that many things in Chania were not as plain as the day that was beginning around me.

The above evening and the memory it evoked illustrate a number of issues I explore in this work: competitive performances, both verbal and somatic, whether over the gaming table or behind it, or between insiders and outsiders; visibility as a marker of activities both illicit and socially tolerated (even revered); and indeterminacy (of the outcomes of the games themselves, of social interactions, and of these performances) as a constant aspect and discursive subject of everyday experience. The uncertainties Nondas confronted on a failed night both at the table and at the helm of a newly acquired business, those Yorgos engaged by the risk of challenging a fair-haired foreigner as he helped himself to a chair at the blackjack table, and those that are manifest in how the owners of Chania's seemingly obvious gambling dens nonetheless sought to control their potentially hazardous exposure to prying eyes—all these uncertainties are linked by the various ways in which Chaniots (those who live in Chania) account for the outcomes that follow them, ways that themselves refer both to more local and to more global kinds of signification, from an appeal to a kind of bad luck to an appeal to statistical probabilities. The varying ways Chaniots talk about and confront uncertainty and unexpected outcomes often entail linking those within the context of gambling to those outside it, making use of the embodied character of many gambling practices and playing on the recurring themes of inclusion or exclusion and secrecy or display in the local illegal gambling practices of Chania.

In the early to mid-nineties, regional crises and environmental hazards rendered economic life in Chania precarious for its roughly 70,000 inhabitants. Most Chaniots involved in the tourist industry pointed to 1991, the summer after the Gulf War, as the low point in this respect, and worried that the violence in the former Yugoslavia, occurring at the time of my research, would create the same problem. A more general sense of fluctuation in tourist levels from year to year permeated tourist business in Chania and was to me the second most frequently cited uncertainty in business, the first being the tax system, which was also undergoing significant change at the time. In the midst of this increased prominence of indeterminacy in day-to-day life I found that Chaniots drew on a largely shared set of concepts for making sense of and confronting the vagaries of political transitions, economic fluctuations, social tensions, personal crises, and the games themselves. The sources of the unpredictability in these domains at times transcended local, regional, and national processes, such as in the notoriously capricious global tourist industry, a mainstay of many Chaniots' economic life, or in the equally important local agricultural industry, where suddenly cheaper prices for South American frozen orange juice (a major competitor of Crete on the European market) can have repercussions that are felt from the city to the countryside. Traditional academic approaches to understanding how people confront such risk invoke probability theory and claims about rationality, often narrowing the stakes of any social action to that which is quantifiable. I contend that these numerous indeterminacies—from those of rolling dice to running a business to confronting local opinion to broader existential insecurities—pervade social life in Chania as elsewhere, and the means to answer the limitations of such conventional approaches lies in understanding both what is at stake (Kleinman and Kleinman 1991) for actors on this shifting ground and how they account for and engage these unpredictabilities. The question of what is at stake takes on a literal meaning in the context of gambling, but it is the combination of material and social stakes risked in the formalized context of a game that provides insight into how Chaniots confront the exigencies of experience more generally. The rules and conventions of different games provide a semistructured context for continuous unpredictable outcomes (dice rolls, hands of cards), so I focus on gambling because this is an activity where risk and indeterminacy are most visibly engaged, talked about, and embodied. Because Chaniots regard gambling as distinct from the rest of everyday life but also as a place where the stakes of the game often entail direct social consequences, and often use the metaphor of gambling to describe social circumstances, gambling is an apt activity in which to explore how social actors confront the unpredictable in general.[5]

The presence of contingency—and how to account for it—has become an increasing concern in attempts to understand such "modern" phenomena as the apparent yet seemingly cryptic volatility of what was briefly called the "new economy" (which appears to transcend national and cultural boundaries, particularly in the case of tourism), the use of randomness by nation-states to enforce policy, and the competing assessments of environmental and health risks by experts and laypeople. Amid this increasing interest in the unpredictable in both academic and popular circles in the West (framed most often as a problem of risk perception or analysis), I here use the everyday activity of gambling in the city of Chania as providing a unique lens through which to explore how social actors confront uncertainty in several key areas of their lives, including illness and mortality, business, and locale or nation-state relations. These unpredictabilities in Chaniot lives arise, I argue, from different sources (such as the ineffable nature of public opinion, the chaotic qualities of complex systems, and the risk of failure in any social action). Furthermore, confronting them necessarily involves struggles over meaning and resources, and thus I argue also for recognition and examination of these struggles, which I call the politics of contingency. My aim here is not only to show how Chaniots account for unexpected events but also to introduce a more comprehensive approach for our explorations of this subject in other locales and to call attention to how particular ways of accounting for unanticipated individual events are themselves implicated in positions of power, practice, and knowledge.[6] A clear example of this on the national scale was the claim by the nationally famous Greek archeologist Manolis Andronikos that the timing of his nationalist-interpreted discoveries at Vergina, in Greek Macedonia, aligned auspiciously with the Greek Orthodox calendar (see Hamilakis and Yalouri 1999 for a discussion of this and similar incidents). Such "accountings" for the unexpected are made necessary by the continual project of maintaining political legitimacy over time. Because an ineradicable uncertainty pervades (institutional) experience through time, I assert, claims to durable political legitimacy must be endlessly propped up to recreate legitimacy anew.

This work thus runs in nearly direct opposition to the general tendency in the social sciences to view the chaotic disruptions and vagaries of life as inherently troubling or anxiety-producing, an approach that has led to a valorizing of the concept of risk management and of those who use it as a formalizing solution to the possibility of the unexpected.[7] Concurrent with this tendency has been the attribution of a worldview of paralyzing fatalism to those who do not use the concept of risk, a practice in which, unfortunately, anthropologists also have played a hand, as I discuss in the next section. Instead, one of my aims in this book is to establish an approach toward indeterminacy that situates the moral attributes of chance as ascribed within the particular circumstances of its appearance. Simply put, to improve our treatment of indeterminacy we must cease to assume that it is dangerous and that those who appeal to interpretations not based on risk assessment are stuck in the past.

Fate, Rationality, and Modernity

As it happens, the ethnographic literature on Greece provides a clear example of this pernicious problem, with its frequent reliance on fate (*mira*) as a descriptive and analytic concept (in part this may result from its longstanding presence in academic approaches toward ancient Greek culture). This concept, given its weighty legacy, can subsume other related but distinct concepts such as luck and chance under the rubric of an overarching, singular cosmology of fate, obscuring the intricacy of Greek attitudes toward the unpredictable, both in the present and the future. From Campbell's description of the links between fate, ancestral sin, and individual will among the Sarakatsani (Campbell 1964, 329–31) to its use by Hart in her work on religion and local historicized identity in the eastern Peloponnese (Hart 1992), this interplay between a "written" and unchangeable destiny and the exercise of individual will has been a recurring theme, but it is one that masks the multiplicity of tropes used by Greeks when referring to the emerging present in the context of an indeterminate future.[8] The overall pattern here is one that neglects other, competing ways in which Greeks make sense of the unpredictable character of existence and thereby also ignores the layers of indeterminacy that pervade social life. It is the literature's emphasis on history, combined with the powerful metaphor of writing that pervades references to fate in Greece, that has led some ethnographers of Greece to overlook two crucial points: the importance of an indefinite future in everyday discourse and action in Greece and the plurality of tropes that Greeks invoke to tie this future to the unfolding present.

In James Faubion's *Modern Greek Lessons* (1993), although he argues for a similarly pervasive awareness of uncertainty in Greece ("doubt," in Faubion's terms, 1993, 5–7), he maintains that it is the distinctive purview of the cultural elite, those who have had the most interaction with the non-Greek world. According to Faubion, these elites have crossed the "threshold of modernity"; that is, they have recognized the possibility that the cosmos could be morally and ethically neutral, that coherent and comprehensive moral and ethical cosmologies may actually be incomplete (1993, 6). This insight provides the impetus for these elites to "renovate" the present through a distinctively eclectic use of the past (Faubion's "historical constructivism"). In this Weberian view, then, this kind of reflective uncertainty is a feature of modernity, and we are left to assume that for those not yet across the threshold there is no doubt in how the world is to be understood, no ability to recognize certain cosmologies as partial or incomplete. However, this argument is at odds with other ethnographies, such as that of J. K. Campbell (1964), where a compelling religious atmosphere among the Sarakatsani shepherds he studies does not erase a fundamental doubt about social judgment, or Herzfeld's *Poetics of Manhood* (1985), where the constant threat of ridicule provides the context for the innovative refiguring of social norms through individual manipulation of history and rhetorical forms. Faubion's argument seems instead to lead to the dichotomy of risk and fate that reproduces a discourse that divides peoples into the rational modern and the irrational premodern.

Similarly, approaches to understanding human action in the context of uncertainty based on narrow conceptions of individual economic self-interest and rationality lead to a limited picture of human life when brought to bear on certain forms of everyday activity. A common sight at the large cafés on the harbor in Chania is that of a few waiters, their work done for the moment, standing close together as two of them flip coins, quickly covering the result. They then exchange a few words—one is calling whether the two coins will be the same (two "heads," *kefalia,* or two "letters," *grammata*) or different—after which both reveal their coins, the winner happily snatching the loser's coin away. It seems a fair distance to travel from this practice to microeconomic theory, but just this kind of game is discussed in a standard introductory text on the subject, in the section introducing decision making under uncertainty (Nicholson 1985, 193–231). The principal strand of economic theory relies on rational choice theory (RCT) in its attempt to understand human decision making under uncertainty.[9] In reference to games such as the coin-flipping game (in economic theory terms, it is an "actuarially fair game"), Nicholson's RCT-based appraisal of them leads him to conclude (Nicholson 1985, 195), "People are generally unwilling to play" them, an observation that flies in the face of the near-ubiquitous playing of this game in Chania's old town.[10] It is only in a footnote that Nicholson recognizes the limits of this approach when attempting to understand social practice (195n): "The games discussed here are assumed to yield no utility in their play other than the prizes: hence the observation that many individuals gamble at 'unfair' odds . . . is not necessarily a refutation of this statement. Rather, such individuals can reasonably be assumed to be deriving some utility from the circumstances associated with the play of the game." RCT-based approaches lead analysts to assume that individuals will not pursue activities that yield no utility in their play. Yet when presented with counterexamples, RCT must effectively shrug its shoulders and point to context, something necessarily excluded by its overly formal approach. It is the importance of these "circumstances" (often not quantified or easily quantifiable—as, for example, in other potential sources of indeterminacy apart from the purely stochastic) that an RCT approach fails to capture. The principal failing of RCT is that, by accounting only for the formal features of the game and its stakes, it necessarily entails a separation of the game and its players' actions and decisions from the local social, cultural, and historical contexts. Unable to account for actors' interests that are not formalizable under its system, RCT is unable to give a full account of everyday experience.

It bears mention that Mary Douglas (1966), who has long attempted to locate the study of risk as a key issue in social and cultural anthropology, provides another criticism of economic approaches. She and Isherwood argued that material consumption (such as gambling) is constitutive of social relationships rather than merely the result, as economics would have it, of individual needs (Douglas and Isherwood 1978). In a more recent work, Douglas has more pointedly lamented the social sciences' bias toward viewing risk as egocentric:

> When he brackets off culture from his work, the well-intentioned risk analyst has tied his own hands. . . . His method assumes that all humans have the same responses and preferences to uncertainty that are enshrined in a utilitarian philosophy. Instead of objectivity, we find ideological entrenchment. Warm-blooded, passionate, inherently social beings though we think we are, humans are presented in this context as hedonic calculators calmly seeking to pursue private interests. We are said to be risk-aversive, but, alas, so inefficient in handling information that we are unintentional risk-takers; basically we are fools. The charge of irrationality has come home to roost. (1992, 13)

Douglas laments that the primary paradigm we have for examining uncertainty in human experience is the rational choice model, one with its roots deep in the nineteenth century's fascination with numbers (see Hacking 1990).[11] Douglas's work represents an attempt to place risk, disorder, and uncertainty center stage in anthropological analysis.

This is a goal shared by Jackson (1989, 15), who proposes that uncertainty is a universal feature of human experience, arguing that "the anthropologist's preoccupation with regularity, pattern, system, and structure has to be seen as less an objective reflection of social reality than a comment on his personal and professional need for certitude and order."[12] In this respect Jackson's views contrast sharply with the later work of Anthony Giddens (1991, 109–43), who, also writing about risk and fate (and subscribing to the dichotomy as a way of distinguishing societies), suggests that there is something qualitatively distinctive about "Western" society—its "enumerated" quality, its modernity—that accounts for (determines) how risk is confronted therein. Jackson questions this tendency to assume that a concern for statistical order is as prevalent outside the university setting as within it.[13]

Other authors have begun to explore how contingency is an ever-present and central aspect of human experience, and they also argue

against approaches that treat attitudes toward risk as either homoge-
neous across individuals or groups or unchanging over time (Keane 1997
[see especially pp. 208–23]; Becker 1997; Whyte 1997). For them, social
actors are enmeshed within webs of relationships and the flux of ongoing and unexpected events, and these actors' engagement of this contingency, rather than a danger to be avoided, can actually be a sought-out
arena for the constitution of self. In Chania, such arenas are multiple,
and the stakes can be high.

Uncertain Sources

The city of Chania lies on the north coast and toward the western
end of the island of Crete and is a popular tourist destination with its
well-preserved Venetian harbor and the looming, picturesque White
Mountains to the south. But Chania is also a city of commerce, surrounded by broad and fertile plains well-suited to citrus production and
terraced hillsides covered with olive trees. Many Chaniots account for
the prevalence of gambling for significant stakes in Chania by alluding
to the wealth created by the combination of tourist and agricultural in-
dustries, and most Chaniots I came to know had direct, kin-based, or pa-
tronal links to these multiple sources of income. Therefore, it is important to keep in mind throughout much of what follows that the variety
of channels along which capital travels in Chania often contributes to its
evasion of control both by the Greek government (through tax evasion
and other illegal financial activities, such as gambling) and by other members of kinship groups, where often some know of one member's frequent
gambling and others do not.

Gambling is widespread and multiform in Chania, constituting a
significant part of the daily life of many Chaniots. Its various forms include state-sponsored gambling (such as lotteries, instant-win scratch
ticket games,[14] and soccer pools), organizations' raffles (legal and illegal),
illegal electronic games with cash payoffs (video slot, poker, and blackjack machines), illegal local gambling (card playing, dicing, and backgammon for money), and local numbers games (often for large, otherwise
practically unsellable fish). It is most visibly a male practice, but women
gamble as well, mostly in their homes (a practice also noted by Herzfeld,
1991, 181). In the course of my research I observed men gambling (mostly
in coffeehouses) and mixed-gender gambling (in clubs [*leskhes*] and in
homes among families on New Year's Eve). As a man I was not able to
gain entry into the restricted feminine spaces where women-only gambling takes place (in their homes during the day in Chania). (This prac-

tice again highlights the role of visibility in gambling, more specifically the threat, or risk, of exposure that looms continually over the participants as they play illegal and often derided games, as evidenced by the measures that the coffeehouses described earlier took to conceal their interiors.) As a result of this methodological limitation, many of the gambling forms I discuss herein are played nearly exclusively by men. However, I was able to observe and explore some mixed-gender gambling, which takes place in a number of locations (backgammon at youth hangouts [cafés, bars] and team-based card games at clubs). These forms of gambling are examined as a group in chapter 2.

Although most gambling falls into one of the aforementioned categories, Chaniots also gamble on more unusual things. Indeed, a large part of the enjoyment of these ad hoc forms lies in the challenge of fashioning a good, creative game. One well-known (in Chania) character of the nightlife (*tis zois tis nikhtas*), Christoforos, gleefully told me of how he and another gambler, with whom he had played cards for years, often sat across from each other outside a coffeehouse on summer afternoons and bet on which of two plates of candied fruit a fly would land on next. What made it all the better, he said, was that others would see the two of them exchanging money and have no idea why! Because in most (illegal) gambling in Chania the game is visible and the incriminating money is not (with the exception of dice, where the gambling space itself is carefully concealed), Christoforos, in the action itself and in the story's telling, used an ironic inversion that made the game invisible and the money visible. Thus he invoked both the closed quality of the gamblers' community (where spectators are viewed not only as not fully understanding what is going on but also as passive receptacles for the performances of the players, such as in my reception at the blackjack table earlier) and their disdain for the need to keep the illegal part of the activity (the exchange of money) hidden. This theme of exposure and concealment is particularly relevant to a discussion of gambling because a primary feature of taking a risk entails exposing oneself to unexpected or unintended consequences (Giddens 1984). This concern with display and concealment in Greece has also been recognized repeatedly in its ethnographic literature (Campbell 1964; du Boulay 1974; Hirschon 1981; Herzfeld 1987, 1991; Cowan 1990) and in this study helps draw attention to how gambling in Chania is simultaneously a potential site for the competitive establishment or legitimation of hierarchy and a potentially embarrassing practice to be hidden from the scrutiny of outsiders.

As mentioned earlier, Chaniots often make the metaphoric link between gambling and risks in life more generally, and this link is also not made only in gambling situations. In matters as diverse as business, kinship and sociability, health, the environment, and politics, choices and events often are framed in terms of games, gambles, and risks. This is evident in the often-heard phrase, usually in reference to national politicians, "They're playing games at our expense" ("*mas pezune pekhnidhia*"; see also Sutton 1997, 431n) and in the even more common "Life is a risk (gamble)!" ("*I zoi ine risko*"), heard most often when reflecting on such tragic events as traffic accidents and forest fires. In making this link, Chaniots manipulate many possible rhetorical forms and concepts available to them (and thereby also create new ones), and making sense of this verbal and nonverbal performance constitutes a large part of this work. For example, it would be a mistake to speak of Chaniots as having a single view of luck.[15] Not only is it just one element in the constellation of concepts that emerge in gambling events, but it also can be invoked in drastically different ways. Luck (both good and bad) can be, variously, inherent in an individual, brought by a friend, identified with an item or place or time, divinely bestowed, or associated with sexual purity. Its efficacy or existence may also simply be denied. Statistical probability, skill, and fate are other parts of this constellation of tropes of accountability that often emerge in gambling and other risk-laden situations. It is the complexity and contingent nature of such concepts, and how through their use local actors both construct and situate themselves in momentarily structured patterns of outcomes, that I explore in this work with the aim of providing a more precise language for our own examinations of the place of chance in experience in Greece and elsewhere.

It is not only the various ways of talking about unexpected outcomes that call for exploration, however. The unpredictabilities of human life are not all cut from the same cloth. To speak usefully about indeterminacy itself, we must distinguish its various sources because the social sciences have labored under unquestioned ideas about chance and probability since the rise of statistical thinking at least (Hacking 1975). My attempt at such clarification therefore is similar to that of Alasdair MacIntyre in *After Virtue* (MacIntyre 1984, 93–105), where he argues for four sources of unpredictability in human life.[16] Very briefly summarized, he recognizes such unpredictabilities as the advent of radical innovation, the impossibility of knowing another's point of view, the inherent complexity of situations that carry a profusion of contributing factors, and pure contingency itself. In my own formulation I also distinguish four sources of indeterminacy, although somewhat differently. This set is not meant as a taxonomy or a necessarily exhaustive list. Furthermore, each kind may overlap or combine with another. In that sense, parsing them in this way is a means of drawing attention to how different circumstances in social life, though all uncertain, are uncertain in different ways. To differentiate between these sources of indeterminacy is to open the way to a serious exploration of how social actors may confront them differently (avoiding blanket assumptions about "risk aversion," for example), and how social standing may depend on demonstrated facility with one or both of them. It also, and perhaps more importantly, aids us in avoiding the hidden moral attributions that lie behind the use of, for example, "risk" or "fate." In this respect, it is also important to reiterate that my approach does not presuppose the normative primacy of order over disorder; it departs from most social science by not assuming uncertainty necessarily to be a problem or source of anxiety.

The first source of indeterminacy is the one perhaps most prominent in academic thinking on the subject. This is the contingency that is the result of stochastic processes, such as dice rolls, distributions of cards from a well-shuffled deck, or other forms of random allotment (MacIntyre calls this "pure contingency"; 1984, 99–100). These results often are amenable to statistical manipulation, and such processes characterize many of the forms of gambling favored by institutions (such as casinos) and nation-states; these include lotteries, scratch ticket games, slot machines, roulette wheels, and "wheels of fortune." An overemphasis on this source as standing for all indeterminacies has led political and academic forms of knowledge about contingency into a valorization of statistical reasoning (Hacking 1990).

Yet uncertainty in most gambling situations does not arise solely from the unpredictable distributions of rolls of the dice and hands of cards. Chance of another kind is inherent in any game or situation where people strategize against each other, where a player attempts simultaneously to apprehend others' intents without revealing his or her own. Thus, the claims Chaniots make at the gaming table often have at least as much to do with public sociability and individual identities as with the capriciousness of the cards or dice. "How can you know another?" (*"Pou na kseris ton allon?"*) was a question I heard often in Chania, and this kind of social indeterminacy lies at the heart of much gambling, a point underscored to me by the many gamblers who nonetheless claimed to be able to read other players' styles, intents, and resources with ease.

In another sense, a third source of indeterminacy is present at the gaming table (and, I argue, beyond it), one that resides between the formal indeterminacy of the cards and the social indeterminacy of reading others' points of view. This is the possibility of failing in the execution of an expressive action, such as when making any of the meaningful statements and gestures in gambling. Stumbling over one's words when grandly pronouncing another's chances to be poor, or moving to slap a backgammon piece resoundingly on the board only to have it bounce off the table and roll weakly across the floor, often result in harsh ridicule, and this possibility of failure renders any social action a risky business.[17] This performative indeterminacy also encompasses the failure to give indications that one is able to observe and follow, or "read," the game, as in backgammon (*tavli*), where being able to "see" the strategic possibilities on the board takes teaching and practice.

Forms of gambling in Chania that are not characterized by contest between local actors, such as state-sponsored games, highlight a different issue and another source of indeterminacy. Here the complex relationships between the Greek person, local community, and state come to the fore. The games are of three types: lotteries (several kinds), a soccer pool, and scratch ticket games.[18] Because Chaniots often frame the Greek state as grasping, corrupt, and incompetent, the games it sponsors are necessarily suspect, seen as yet another way in which the government steals from the populace. But they also provide, through the real and immediate possibility of winning, an opportunity to gain a material benefit from the state ("without working for it," as one inveterate player of scratch ticket games characterized it). In this respect the common practice of tax evasion in Greece has many similarities with playing the state games.[19] Resistance to structures of domination such as the state, and the conviction that one can "get around" its demands (in Greek, *elisete*, which implies moving around obstacles like a snake), bring into relief the potential for doubt when confronting any ideology sponsored by an institution, such as the purported consistency, efficiency, and power of the nation-state. This indeterminacy is of the same kind that Faubion recognized: the potential for cosmologic doubt. This cosmologic indeterminacy comes most clearly into focus through the classic social science question of theodicy, when a belief system is taken to task for its inability to provide a moral justification either for desultory suffering or for good fortune falling on those deemed immoral (see Weber 1930; Herzfeld 1992). Thus, the question of theodicy lies, one could say, at the intersection between moral evaluation and chance and suggests that the completeness of any cosmology can be called into doubt.[20]

It is this complex interplay between different forms of gambling, the contingent use of concepts pertaining to chance, the risks and uncertainties in social life, and the interplay of unpredictability across such spheres from one moment to the next that I examine in the chapters to follow. To reiterate, this set of sources of indeterminacy thus includes the *formal indeterminacy* of discrete chance events, often amenable to quantification in aggregation (such as rolls of the dice, distributions of cards, and series of these but also more catastrophic events, such as illness or accident), the *social indeterminacy* of the fundamentally elusive nature of others' points of view (encompassing the indeterminacy of language and gesture, however felicitously performed), the *performative indeterminacy* involved in the execution of a performative act (that it be done well or poorly; Austin's notion of "felicity"), and the *cosmologic indeterminacy* by which explanatory systems can be called into doubt (such as in the question of theodicy).

As people move through their lives, they confront moments of possibility that we may usefully view as arising from these various unpredictabilities, and each of the games I discuss reveals different aspects of how Chaniots make sense of them. Thus, Nondas, the owner of the coffeehouse lacking business on its potentially biggest night, was presented in the midst of this outcome with his own lack of success at the poker table. The realms of business and poker share a deep concern with concealing and revealing intentions and strategies while calling for a mastery of reading the opinions and intents of one's adversaries (or customers). For Nondas's situation, it seems that poker provided an appropriate resource in his (and others') attempts to account for what was happening to him. By contrast, backgammon as played in Chania involves a contest of two players amid public scrutiny, and its structure invites links with sociability and courtship and kin relations. State-sponsored gambling serves as an arena for making sense of a different kind of relationship, that between the individual and the state, and Chaniots thus associate it with the practice of tax evasion, the preeminent forum for individual versus state conflict. Finally, dice gambling pits the individual player less against other players or the state as it does against the fickle currents of chance itself, where fortunes rise and fall rapidly and where Chaniots link their struggles to engage this caprice with their professed ability to face their own mortality.

But what does this examination of moments of unpredictability reveal about the flow of time and social change? The temporal dimension to this issue of risk merits further emphasis, for although anthropology has recently attended to the uses of history, how stances toward the future are used has received less attention; I suggest that the unfolding of outcomes such as occurs in gambling provides not only a window on how actors position themselves vis-à-vis the future but also links that future to an emerging present and a contested past. In this sense, claims about past, present, and future outcomes are not simply about prediction and control, as traditional economic approaches might suggest, but rather entail a construction of reality with reference to the favorable or unfavorable position of the claimant or others. In this work, then, I attempt to answer the question with which Weber was so concerned: How do people make sense of, in his telling phrase, the "distribution of fortune" in the world (Weber 1946, 271, 275)? What is at stake over the gambling table is not solely the money on the table and the social status of the participants: Reality itself is up for grabs (along with the players' places in it), shaped amid the structures and conventions of the games, the unfolding of shifting outcomes, and in terms of chance, luck, skill, and fate—tropes that implicate not simply the bounded chance of the cards and dice but also the local social world of the participants.[21]

Following Fernandez, who characterizes the play of tropes as a "predication upon an inchoate situation" (1986, 8), a way of accounting for something otherwise ambiguous, I use the phrase "trope of accountability" to refer to each of these ways—fate, luck, probability, purity—of accounting for the indeterminate, the continuously shifting ground of unfolding outcomes. This is a departure from the formal, semiotic usage of "trope," but it is consistent with more common academic usage. The advantages of speaking in terms of tropes are that it both points to the performative aspects of their use and places them on the same ontological level. I also refer to encounters with unpredictability in any of its manifestations as "engagements of chance," for this phrase avoids an overemphasis on an actor's ability or intention to control or predict the unfolding present (and future) and also avoids a subordination of the actor to the whims of chaotic (and yet, ironically, thereby determinative) contingencies. This "chance engagement" reflects gambling's potency as a metaphor for everyday experience, as players confront and engage the game, or life itself with all of its vagaries, as much as they do each other.

Bodies at Stake

The language of tropes runs one risk of its own, however, and that is an overemphasis on verbal performance at the expense of nonverbal components of social action. The issue of embodiment, explored in relation to Greek dance by Cowan (1990), has a similar importance in gambling because gestures and comportment are viewed as revealing aspects of one's strategy and situation in the game (as well as of one's character in other contexts). One card game in Chania, though rarely played, illustrates this emphasis on bodily expression. *Skabili* ("slap," itself a corporeally evocative name) consists of two teams of three players each (seated alternately). There is a period where a trump suit is determined through bidding, after which tricks are taken, as in bridge. What makes this game unusual is that on each team the players try to communicate with their partners, through gestures, which of the trump cards they have, without giving this information away by letting the other side see the signals. The gestures are standardized and consist of small, quick movements. Having the ace, for example, is communicated by winking (see the appendix for a fuller account of this game and others encountered in and around Chania). Here the skill of reading others' bodies is especially foregrounded, but it is an issue that recurs in all the games I examine here. The exposed quality of much corporeal performance provides a further opportunity to engage performative indeterminacy. Pierre Bourdieu (1977) suggests that the embodied nature of social experience is fundamental to understanding social action, and this is particularly true for gambling, which, because of the rules and conventions active at any moment, provides regular opportunities for similar gestures.

The playing with the conventionality of such rules in particular situations, an aspect of the poetics of social practice, is addressed by Bourdieu (1977, 7) in his discussion of tempo, that is, how one can manipulate the timing of one's actions to create meaning, an idea that provides a further source of insight for a consideration of game-playing activity specifically. In the case of a game called *thanasis*, for example, proper timing can draw attention to one's actions and highlight an important moment, as I observed one evening at a coffeehouse near the central market of Chania (agora). *Thanasis* is played by four to seven players and involves each player in turn drawing a card from the deck (or discard pile) and either discarding it or exchanging it for one of the ten cards in hand. This continues until one player has the proper assortment of cards to win the game.[22] A rhythm develops quickly as players draw and discard one after the other, one player drawing from the deck almost before the previous player's discard has landed (although not before that player has checked to see whether it is a desirable card). On this night, the players, when drawing from the face-down deck spread slightly across the green felt, were pulling the top card toward them with the tips of their fingers, often flicking up a corner of it on the way to check, all the more quickly, whether it was the card they wanted. One player, Manolis, was in the midst of doing this when he changed direction, pushing the card in a circle around the deck. The sudden change in rhythm seemed to bring all of the players up with a start; the next player in particular seemed held up, with his hand halfway to the pile in anticipation. "Change! Change, bastard!" (*"Allakse! Allakse, moreh!"*), Manolis entreated as he circled the deck three times, after which he casually flipped the card face-up on the table. It was a joker, a wild card, and he laid the rest of his cards next to it to prove he now had a winning hand. The games I explore throughout this work are saturated with such opportunities to delay or strike quickly, again within the context of conventions and rules, and successful performances can impressively elide, if only briefly, the boundaries between random allotments and personal power, as in this case.

Timothy Jenkins (1994) explores the link between this practical aspect of experience and the domain of social indeterminacy. Drawing on the work of Bourdieu (1977) and Herzfeld (1987), Jenkins suggests that the conditions of fieldwork have crucial similarities with everyday experience, and he focuses on a single ethnographic example, that of buying and selling cattle in southwestern France. (It is worthwhile to note that buying and selling cattle involves a "contest of wills" between the two parties, much like the contests of manhood or self-esteem that characterize much gambling in Chania.) Jenkins argues that the acquiring of Bourdieu's "habits for action" that is a part of being a member of society is also true for the anthropologist; that is, his or her experience of coming to know how to act is not qualitatively different from the same experience for local actors. This practical quality to everyday life has implications for any attempt to understand gambling that relies on models of rule-governed behavior as well, such as the rational choice model discussed earlier. As Jenkins (1994, 439) writes, "If much social life is practical rather than theoretical, embodied in habits and 'dispositions,' behavior is not made up of rule-governed responses to stimuli, but rather is constructed or improvised on the basis of these habits that enable actors to generate an infinite number of practices adapted to constantly changing situations." Jenkins continues, asserting that "recourse to language in any contact or context raises the question of what is at stake" (446; see also Kleinman and Kleinman 1991), and suggests that this very indeterminacy of meaning is not exclusively a challenge to the anthropologist; it is true of the experience of all the actors involved, an aspect highlighted further when the practice is gambling, where issues of indeterminacy are placed center stage. Other writers have commented on the centrality of disorder in the ad hoc formation of meaning, most often in the context of language and metaphor (Fernandez 1986; Friedrich 1986; Herzfeld 1993; Keane 1997). The key here is that the semantic ambiguity of gesture and language is the central component of social indeterminacy, where one is confronted with the fundamental doubt about knowing others' points of view.

This example also provides an example of an approach to indeterminacy that is at first not obvious. Instead of concerning oneself with squaring the outcomes in a gambling situation with one's place amid them through the use of one trope of accountability or another, many gamblers prefer to present themselves as completely unconcerned about these outcomes, placing themselves above the fray, as it were. This "instrumental nonchalance" is a difficult pose to put into practice, as it is the presentation of a subtle but unbreakable manifest conviction that neither favorable nor unfavorable results are important, a seamless unflappability. In a way, this is a kind of performance of nonperformance, as it is a resolute refusal to play along, so to speak, but one that is paradoxically effective in bringing about preferable results. This stance becomes particularly poignant in the face of mortality, as I discuss in chapter 6.

Rethinking Uncertainty

In attempting to place gambling center stage as a practice and do the same for indeterminacy as an issue in everyday social life, I am concerned with avoiding a reduction of the social practices surrounding gambling and chance to one discourse or another. I oppose the view that pits risk against a fatalistic view of experience; rather, I see risk as the engagement of one or more of these sources as grounded in social action, exposing to gain or loss one's symbolic capital (Bourdieu 1989). In this view, engagements of chance include not only the explicit placing of bets in the course of games but also claims about the unfolding of outcomes made in those games and other activity in the context of the game that is open to the scrutiny of others. Thus the tropes of accountability that Chaniot gamblers use become a set of ways in which they and other Chaniots attempt to situate themselves and others amid a shifting field of potential influences, influences that can affect everything from dice rolls, to the number of tourists visiting Chania in a given year, to the health of Greece's prime minister.

Therefore, it is the concurrent and combined use of varied and variable tropes of chance (whether statistical probability, fate, luck, skill, or nonchalance) that I address, attempting further to relate the claims made through these tropes to the pervasive indeterminacies of experience. I intend thereby to demonstrate the need to incorporate an understanding of social performance into an area previously seen as quintessentially economic and begin to outline how risk in Greece and elsewhere, rather than tamed and quantified, is engaged and performed. As a consequence of this emphasis on social action in the making and also as a part of my efforts to protect the identities of contacts engaged in illegal (though often tolerated) activities, I do not focus on gamblers' life histories or on their own reflective narratives of their experiences. There are places where these kinds of data play a role, but for the most part, this book follows the action (to use an appropriate piece of American gambling slang).

Although the worldwide prevalence of various kinds of gambling—state sponsored, legal nonprofit (such as raffles), legal commercial (casinos), and illegal—and the abundance of images of gamblers in the global media[23] suggest that gambling is a significant part not only of human activity but also of how people talk about themselves and others, treatment of the issue in the ethnographic literature has been spotty at best. Gambling has been mentioned in several ethnographies of Greece, but it has not been the exclusive focus of any study. Herzfeld (1985, 1991) has argued that sheep stealing and other economic activities (including gambling) in rural Crete provide a context for the formation of social relationships and for contests of identity and manhood through social performance. In her study of dance in a town in northern Greece, Cowan (1990, 135–70) describes a *lahio* (a raffle or lottery), held as a part of a dance sponsored by a local Businesspeople's Association, where the prizes are items donated by local businesses. Beyond Greece specifically, the most extensive subset of the anthropological literature on gambling has seen it as a means by which to redistribute unequal incomes and as a forum for building exchange relationships (see, for example, Zimmer 1986, 1987). However, none of the studies following this approach treats the risk inherent in investment as central to the activity, nor do they see this economic activity as a site where ideas about uncertainty are revealed and negotiated. Instead, they create a functional interpretation of gambling as a cultural practice, arguing that it serves the needs of the community to share risk and wealth. More recently, works that look at gambling and risk taking in alternative ways have begun to appear, and include, for example, a study of the lives of lottery winners (Falk and Mäenpää 1999). Although this literature on gambling in anthropology is still a work in progress, there are two prominent, and in one case famous, examinations of gambling that resonate clearly with what I observed in Chania, and they provide a pair of key insights applicable for studying gambling in any context.

It is impossible to avoid here a consideration of one of the most well-known (and most thoroughly discussed) articles in the anthropological literature: Geertz's "Deep Play: Notes on the Balinese Cockfight" (Geertz 1973, 412–53).[24] Several of the features of Balinese cockfighting that Geertz describes are consistent with dice gambling in Chania. In both places, it seems, it is identified with special occasions, it often serves as a metaphor for other spheres of social life ("Court trials, wars, political contests, inheritance disputes, and street arguments are all compared to cockfights" [418]), the stakes can be very high, for certain gamblers the practice becomes obsessive, it is for men only, and there is a performative auction or bazaar where bets are entreated and accepted. These similarities aside, Geertz's treatment of the event is tied more closely to his broader thesis that cultural activity is a text to be read than to the distinctive aspect of cockfighting and gambling—that is, its indeterminacy. In addressing an activity that highlights uncertainty he transforms it into a static appraisal of extant social structures. In his formulation, cockfighting is art, and art is solely an expression of "the social matrix" (436).[25] He thereby imbues the local social organization with (unchanging) certainty by treating a locus of unpredictability as art.

Although Geertz recognizes that in the cockfight "much more is at stake than material gain: namely, esteem, honor, dignity, respect—in a word . . . status" (433), he continues, "It is at stake symbolically, for (a few cases of ruined addict gamblers aside) no one's status is actually altered by the outcome of a cockfight" (433). This statement rests on an assumed distinction between symbolic and material interests, and I suggest that it thereby puts up obstacles to gaining a better understanding of the ongoing and processual nature of social life in the flow of time. Despite the overall nuanced nature of Geertz's description, he excludes from his statement the "addicts" who have suffered "real consequences," but in what way is being labeled an addict not a "real consequence" of a gambling event? Geertz does not explore the potentially variable meanings of a cultural category as attributed in different contexts—that is, how the attribution of addiction, in this case, may serve local interests rather than be an unquestionable index of certain actors' personalities. It also seems that, in Geertz's formulation, either the actors themselves do not realize that nothing is being risked or they engage in gambling only to see their own social matrix expressed. It seems more likely that gamblers who insist that they are risking nothing (read: nothing important) are making their own claims to status by distancing themselves from monetary concerns, much as Chaniot gamblers boast about their losses rather than their gains ("Yes, I lost $600 dollars, but it means nothing to me").

However, there is a deeper issue that is also relevant for any examination of gambling, which Geertz points to, and that is *how* a gambler wins or loses, or what might be called the poetics of risk taking.[26] According to Geertz (1973, 439), betting practices often follow the principles of segmentary opposition, and he gives some indications that how a gambler handles "cross-loyalty situations" (how he bets "against the grain" or avoids relatives and friends or avoids betting altogether) can have real consequences. The poetics of gambling—in formal terms, how one can manipulate the form of an action to enhance the content or meaning of it—constitutes a crucial component of any examination of gambling (or taking risks more generally) precisely because of the risk inherent in making a claim performatively, exposing one's action to the scrutiny of others. The tropes and gestures one uses to make sense of the shifting outcomes and resources in a gambling event invoke a wide range of meanings, from the formal "rationality" of statistical probability to the fickle whims of local ideas of luck. Geertz's article, nearly thirty years after the fact and despite its limitations, can now be seen to point ahead to some of the key elements of an anthropological approach to the engagement of chance.

Another approach to gambling as a social activity is Oxfeld's (1993) study of a Chinese community in Calcutta. The description Oxfeld gives of the gambling practices is strikingly similar in some respects to gambling in Greece, particularly the generational and gender homogeneity of many gambling groups and how gambling is sanctioned during the week of New Year's celebrations, and her insights into the relationship between business activity and gambling are particularly appropriate to delve into here. She examines how a social group that emphasizes a strict, fiscally conservative, entrepreneurial ethic could often engage in a variety of forms of gambling (1993, 107–20). The study no doubt gains some of its salience by playing on its audience's expectations. Why might we find it incongruous for conservative entrepreneurs also to be furious gamblers? Upon further reflection, this reveals some of the paradoxes inherent in the popular and academic assumptions about economic action in the West and finds resonance in the recent interest in the apparently increased volatility of the "new economy." The seemingly inscrutable and rapid fluctuations in business fortunes associated with it have challenged the conventional assumptions of rationality and equilibrium that have largely characterized the view of Western economics since Adam Smith. It appears that it is no longer sufficient to account for these outcomes by appealing to established business principles, statistical patterns, or the lack of perfect information. Instead, an irreducible indeterminacy may reside in a quintessentially "modern" system often previously assumed to be guided with surety by an "invisible hand." Oxfeld's study confronts this tension head-on and eschews a conventional analytical framework that might see the Chinese entrepreneurs as moving between rational and irrational mentalities. Instead, she gets at the heart of the paradox of risk in economic life: It is simultaneously dangerous and desirable.

Oxfeld notes how her informants, in talking about gambling both directly and as a metaphor for other aspects of social life, invoke the subtly different concepts of luck, skill, and fate, but rather than treat these invocations as contextually contingent, she attempts to make of them a coherent system of attitudes toward gambling, one that also squares with the capitalist activities of her informants. To make further sense of the relationship between business and gambling, Oxfeld first attempts to place gambling activity firmly outside the normal scope of everyday life. She then distinguishes between gambling that is "ordered and bounded—not only in terms of time and place, but even in terms of one's partners" and "compulsive or uncontrolled gambling." But it is difficult not to find this distinction also problematic when Oxfeld notes that, "whereas a successful entrepreneur will rarely be taken to task for his gambling, an unsuccessful one may find his bad luck blamed on a bad habit" (1993, 109).

Oxfeld herself recognizes this problem and struggles to reconcile gambling's simultaneous separation from and connection to an entrepreneurial social life that at times mirrors gambling's concern with luck and fate yet seems concurrently to discount reliance on luck rather than hard work. She concludes,

> Gambling among the Calcutta Chinese, therefore, does not really exist apart from social life. But it may exclude or invert social realities as well as merely reflect them. . . .
>
> Perhaps it is best to see gambling as an expression of the contradictions inherent in their entrepreneurial ethos, an orientation which acknowledges both fate and skill as elements in business success, and which understands the roles of both prudence and risk taking. It is an outlook that gives status to those with the most wealth, but which thereby acknowledges the possibility of shake-ups in the status system when family fortunes change. Finally, while the community's ethos places emphasis on prudence, saving, and wise investment, it also admits that the ultimate aim is to be beyond want. (1993, 119)

Oxfeld portrays clearly the complex relationship between business and gambling, a relationship with similar complexity in Greece. Oxfeld sees gambling as a window into local attitudes toward unpredictability, and in this work I examine corresponding concepts in Chania, thereby situating gambling practices in the context of everyday engagements of chance.

In chapter 1 I consider the settings in which much of Chaniot gambling takes place and introduce the social landscape of Chania and the means by which it and its surrounding prefecture are conceptually divided by Chaniots, layered with ambiguous distinctions much like the practice of gambling itself. Chapters 2–5 are each concerned with particular locations where gambling takes place in Chania and, correspondingly, focus on the games characteristic of those venues. As noted earlier, these games (and the discursive constructions of chance they entail) also provide insight into other uncertain spheres of Chaniot experience (business, sociability, state relations, and mortality). In each of these chapters, then, taking my lead from the connections between games, contexts, tropes, and experience that Chaniots themselves make, I emphasize one or more of these spheres, but this emphasis should not be taken to suggest an overly schematic picture; it is for convenience, and to counteract this tendency I have also endeavored to make connections between chapters. In chapter 2 I consider backgammon (*tavli*) and other games played in contexts where men and women (and children, at times) participate. Backgammon's emphasis on personal contest, where the stakes in monetary terms often are lower but those of status can be high, highlights the tension between luck and skill, as this game more than any other is subject to public view and comment, leading to further instances of relational constructions of gender identities. Another game, *berimba*, a complex and long game that pits pairs of mixed gender (and often married) couples against each other, creates a highly charged atmosphere where accusations of cheating and other breaches of convention are common. Chapter 3 is a discussion of poker as played in Chania's gambling coffeehouses—a game where, as in business, the ability to read others' intentions without revealing your own, as well as tying one's overall fortunes in the game to the immediate social circumstances, are played out in the games themselves and the players' claims about them. In chapter 4 I examine the various forms of state games, most often played in lottery shops, games that in Chania become fodder, like tax collection, for the battle between a suspect and arbitrary state and the clever and indomitable individual or locale. The hidden and often seasonal bars and clubs where the dice game *zaria* is played are the subject of chapter 5, and here the dangerous combination of very high stakes, a 50-50 game, and a bazaar-like atmosphere can lead to ruination or redemption.

I end the work with an intimate portrait of a close friend and contact who died shortly after I left Chania. Although he was an avid backgammon and card player (though for only very small material stakes) and the one who taught me more games than any other contact in Chania, I tell Nikos's story and try to make sense of his death as a way of moving this discussion of contingency beyond the realm of gambling per se. By applying the insights and approach developed throughout the book to this context I seek to demonstrate the value of renovating our ideas about contingency along the lines I suggest, particularly as a way of recognizing how engaging even the uncertainty of an anticipated but unknown death's timing, as he did, can be an opportunity to constitute selfhood by enacting an attitude toward chance.

Notes

1. The name Nondas is a pseudonym, as are those of all other people, places of business, and villages mentioned in this work. The only exceptions are for businesses and places when presented as landmarks within general descriptions of the city and prefecture of Chania. When absolutely necessary I have also altered minor details of some gamblers' profiles to protect their identity.

2. The markers represented approximately 250 Greek drachmas (Dr) each in 1995, or about US$1; the stack of twenty was 5,000 Dr, or about US$20. All values in drachmas throughout the remainder of this work follow this formula for approximation in U.S. dollars. The effects on Greek gambling of the introduction of the euro on January 1, 2001, have not yet been explored.

3. A detailed discussion of *zaria* can be found in chapter five.

4. In Greece, "American" is often used to refer to a returned immigrant to the United States.

5. In this respect Greek gambling shares many characteristics with Greek dance, described by Cowan (1990, 5) as "a site of social action that is both set apart from and embedded in ordinary social relations and meanings."

6. This key issue therefore is similar to that confronted by Sally Falk Moore (1978, 39) in her suggestion that indeterminacy must be accounted for in examinations of the tensions between "the pressure toward establishing and maintaining order and regularity, and the underlying circumstance [of] counter-activities, discontinuities, variety, and complexity [that] make[s] social life inherently unsuited to social ordering." This approach is manifest in James Ferguson's book *The Anti-Politics Machine* (1990, 20), an examination of the "complex relation between the intentionality of planning and the strategic intelligibility of [unintended] outcomes." My project, though sharing a similar goal, differs from this approach in that I examine local discourses about chance and their performance to apprehend indeterminacy's role in local constructions of reality. See chapter 4, however, for an exploration of how state-sponsored gambling in Greece begins to provide the state with a degree of control over these local engagements of chance.

7. One recent work, though sharing this assumption about the inherent negativity of the unexpected in daily life, has nonetheless moved in new directions to begin to examine how social actors themselves make meaning of disruptive events (Becker 1997). For an early and pathbreaking example of this kind of work in the context of medical training, see Bosk (1979).

8. Even the most engaging and illuminating discussion of how attributions of fatalism are part of a larger project of describing and justifying a hegemonic discourse on Greece does not address this other side of the struggle over the present—the use of various stances toward the future—concentrating instead on fate as a key orienting concept for Greek attitudes toward the past (Herzfeld 1987, 37–39). But see Herzfeld's discussion of divination in another work (1985, 247–58,

but especially p. 257), where he asserts that the fundamentally uncertain quality of the future is a key component in the meanings gleaned through scapulomancy.

9. The reliance on the concept of "rationality" has led to much critical scrutiny from a number of different quarters, and I will not replicate those arguments in full here. See, for example, Wilson 1970, Godelier 1972, Tambiah 1990, Anand 1993, Green and Shapiro 1994, and Good 1994.

10. Similarly, Lichtenstein and Slovic (1971) found in their observations of gamblers in Las Vegas that standard economic models were of very limited use for describing or predicting their behavior.

11. In Douglas's view, the response to risk characteristic of a culture is a direct result of the social structure of that culture. Specifically, it is the amount of "solidarity" in the society that determines how it deals with risk and blame: "There are communities, barely earning the name, which are not organized at all: here blame goes in all directions, unpredictably. . . . In short, the stronger the solidarity of a community, the more readily will natural disasters be coded as signs of reprehensible behavior" (1992, 6). This approach, with its strong Durkheimian tenor, though clearly a contrast to the egocentric models Douglas criticizes, nonetheless goes too far in that it erases local interests of the actors involved in gambling events. Instead, I suggest a view that considers the range of local discourses about chance and risk, examining how they are used by particular individuals themselves situated amid local obligations and struggles.

12. Insight into the roots of the phenomenon Jackson notes may be found in the work of science historian Ian Hacking (1975, 1990). Hacking has examined the changing meanings of such related concepts as chance, probability, and indeterminacy in Europe over the last several hundred years. In broad outline, he argues that the creation of statistical theory and the corresponding explosion of statistical research on society in the nineteenth century allowed the "enumeration of society," both in the amount of statistical research on people and in the degree to which numbers began to permeate people's everyday lives. This led to the replacement, he argues, of the idea of "human nature," the hallmark of the enlightenment, with the concept of (statistical) "normalcy," and "normal people" (Hacking 1990, 160–69). The (European) social world was no longer determined, but it was not wholly chaotic. Instead, statistics had tamed chance and had offered statistical laws as a means of prediction (and control) (Hacking 1990). This supplanting of social determinism opened the way for an entrepreneurial class to begin to dominate social and political discourse through their emerging power based on these new methods of predicting and controlling human behavior. It is with this as the backdrop that the current popular and academic ideas of chance and uncertainty discussed earlier must be considered. Hacking's work suggests that the emphasis on prediction and statistics is the result of a particular intellectual tradition rather than an a priori human response to uncertainty.

13. See also the work of James Carrier (1992). He considers Occidentalism in anthropological thought with reference to Mauss's *The Gift* (1990 [1925]) and specifically the problematic distinction of commodity versus gift societies, a discussion of reciprocity easily transferable to the equally problematic distinction of fate (nonmodern) versus risk (modern) societies. See also Douglas and Isherwood's *The World of Goods* (1978, 40) for a further example of this questionable approach.

14. These scratch ticket games are nearly identical to the many such games available from state lottery agencies in the United States. In fact, the tickets used in Greece are made by a U.S. company, printed according to Greek designs and with Greek text.

15. For further discussion of the multiple forms of luck in Chania, see chapters 2 and 3.

16. See also the work of Thomas Csordas (1993). I discuss its connections to my work in another context (Malaby 2002).

17. In the Austinian sense, this is the possibility for performative "infelicities" (Austin 1975 [1956]).

18. Since the time when the bulk of this research was conducted (1994–96) the Greek government has introduced several new games (including a new lottery and another soccer pool) and expanded its scratch ticket offerings.

19. See chapter 4 for a discussion of state games.

20. Dice gambling, though sharing some features with state-sponsored games (such as the straightforward and explicit pitting of individuals against random distributions of chance) nonetheless differs crucially from them because in this illegal and hidden form of gambling there is no overarching institution to come between the gambler and his pursuit of fortune. *Zaria*'s betting system and context also downplay any notions of person-to-person contest such as those found in poker or backgammon, so the game exposes its players all the more starkly to an ongoing presentation (through the rapid outcomes of tossed dice) of their own positions vis-à-vis chance. It is a game that, nearly stripped of social and institutional context, poses a distinct challenge for the social analyst. In this sense, *zaria* places the bounded indeterminacy of the dice themselves side by side with the player's search for meaning—cosmologic indeterminacy—but in this case without an intervening institution. It is a bleak picture, and the description at the start of this introduction begins to communicate it.

21. These tropes are as much about determinacy as about indeterminacy; indeed, that is the crux of the issue here, as they create momentary claims of, if not cause and effect, at least influence. Because they are not lasting, however, and because of a longstanding emphasis on order and regularity in the social sciences, I choose throughout this work to emphasize the lack of ultimate resolution to these claims through the phrase "tropes of accountability."

22. For a complete description of this and other card games, see the appendix.

23. Some of these images include magazine articles on casinos and how to "beat the odds," films that associate panache and heroism with handling oneself in a casino, and novels such as Dostoevsky's *The Gambler* (1972 [1866]). See chapter 5 for comments exploring the link Chaniot dice gamblers make between this novel and their lives.

24. With more extensive discussions of this work and its place in the literature available in other places (Crapanzano 1986; Roseberry 1982), I limit my comments here to how Geertz addresses the gambling component of the cockfight and the broader issue of uncertainty.

25. To be more precise, what the cockfight expresses in Geertz's formulation is unclear, as it is, variously, a representation of the social hierarchy or a "dramatization of status concerns" (436–37); an ordering of themes such as death, masculinity, chance, pride, and beneficence that exposes their "essential nature" (443);

and an indication, through the "vocabulary of sentiment," of the (emotional) building blocks of society and individuals (449). One statement he makes is unequivocal, however: "The cockfight . . . makes nothing happen" (443).

26. This performative quality characteristic of gambling practices has been discussed in the context of other activities in Greece, such as dancing, by Cowan (1990), and sheep-stealing, by Herzfeld (1985). The approaches taken in these ethnographies have served as models for my own research into the performative aspects of Cretan gambling. These works recognize and examine the importance of sociability in Greek life and place the site of much of this activity, the coffeehouse, center stage. This work in part continues this objective, focusing on a familiar aspect of coffeehouse life, gambling, but unlike these works, however, I pursue gambling as an activity not only of the coffeehouse but also of the café, the club, and the lottery shop.

1   *Shifting Ground*

I can walk into fifteen coffeehouses in Chania. I don't go
to just one; I know many people here.

—Nikos

All gamblers have the snout of a pig; they root around for
the money wherever it is to be found. It doesn't matter if
you slept with his wife the night before; if there is money
there, he will come.

—Manolis

And so is framed one of the central puzzles of gambling and
sociability in Chania. Just as a player may state with pride how welcome
he is at any number of gambling coffeehouses, so will another one deride
his willingness to "root around" for the higher-stakes gambling on any
given night, at the expense of any personal dignity. Unraveling the complex web of social ties and personal histories that characterize the community of gamblers in Chania and situating them in their imagined city
landscape is a task never truly completed, but over the course of my time
there certain major lines of contest became apparent. To set the stage for
the chapters to follow, I consider here some of the principal ways in
which Chaniots talk about and distinguish their city and each other.
Contrasts between old and new, city and prefecture, locals and tourists
and military (at the nearby NATO base), among others, shape the social
landscape within which Chaniots, gamblers and nongamblers alike, op-
erate. The social negotiation of the significance or applicability of these
attributions relies on their malleability, the indeterminacy of meaning
where categories are stretched or shifted in the claims of local actors. The
picture of Chania that emerges here is a necessarily incomplete one,

reflecting more a moment in time rather than an eternal portrait, but it has the merit of reflecting the perspective of many of the local gamblers, who themselves point out their partial understanding of this shifting terrain (although often still maintaining its superiority to those of other locales and of institutions). To provide this picture, I begin by focusing on two meeting places and intersections in Chania—Santrivani Square in the old harbor and the agora (public market) on the border between the new and old parts of the city—as a way of introducing Chaniots' ongoing concern with the city's history, both monumental and hidden.

From the coffeehouse to the card-playing club to the private club, two themes emerge that will continue to inform this account of indeterminacy and Chaniot life: the tension between concealment and exposure and the directly related significance of the boundaries that mark relative spheres of intimacy. A further and related theme throughout this chapter (and the work as a whole) is the place of Chania and Crete within local and national struggles over identity, how they are imagined and talked about by Chaniots. A significant issue for Chaniots is their position vis-à-vis the "West," an issue not unique to Chania; the disemic quality of "Greek" identity more generally has been extensively discussed elsewhere.[1] In Chania, concern over the protective boundaries of intimacy that guard potentially embarrassing activities such as gambling exists alongside the historical and other features of the town and prefecture that figure most prominently in references to local identity.

Meetings of Memory and People

Spreading out from the Aegean Sea on the northern coast of Crete, the town of Chania[2] occupies a broad, rolling, and fertile plain before the foothills of the island's western range, the White Mountains. The city itself has a long and varied history, and although its Minoan-era ruins were long buried and nearly obliterated by the town's continued habitation, the periods of Venetian and Ottoman occupation have inscribed themselves on the town indelibly through the largely still extant Venetian walls, which roughly indicate a boundary between the older neighborhoods within, including the Venetian harbor, and the newer neighborhoods and commercial districts stretching into the countryside.

A central location in the old town is Santrivani Square, which borders the water at the northern end of a busy road, Halidon Street, that runs from the surrounding newer parts of Chania down to the old harbor (*palio limani*). In Venetian-era maps showing the layout of the fortress when it was in use, the square can be plainly seen (although its name at the time,

if it indeed had one, is unknown and it is marked only *piazza*, or square),
and during the periods of Venetian and Ottoman rule, when the city was
divided into three sections (the western side for Christians, the eastern
for Muslims, and the center for Jews), the square lay at the meeting point
of these neighborhoods. Today Chaniots still use the name regularly (as
when telling a taxicab driver a destination or arranging a meeting), but
the square itself is currently unmarked by sign or monument (in contrast
to many other squares in the city) and ill-defined; it is a wide, roughly
triangular space connecting the curving stone-paved quay bordering the
water to the street from the new city above. The name of the square
(which is a variant of *sintrivani*, "fountain," because one used to occupy
the center of the square) is now apparent only in a sign for one of the three
large cafés that surround it, Santrivani Café. Colorfully appointed tables
and rattan and wicker chairs stretch out from the small interiors where
coffee is made and meals cooked and encroach on the open space of the
square, but the lack of high buildings around it makes for an easy appraisal
of the curving harbor and the jumble of buildings painted in muted tones
that rise above the water on either side. During the day and evening, especially in the high season (from May to October), tourists continually file
through this narrow mouth and begin to spread out along the harbor on
both sides, solicited constantly by the head waiters of the cafés and restaurants.

Sitting at one of these cafés gives one a sweeping view of the harbor, and they are favored vantage points for locals, who can easily espy
a friend or relative who walks by. On warmer days in the winter the cafés
are filled with locals in the afternoons, particularly on the weekends,
although unlike in many similar cafés in less central locations, one sees
no backgammon played outside. It is played at Koupes, one of the square's
cafés, but only inside the small interior, where it is mostly off-duty waiters and some older friends of the owner who participate. The owner of
Koupes, Stephanos, does not like it to be played outside (in fact, he ex-
pressly forbids it) in view of the tourists or the upper- and middle-class
locals who "come to sit and enjoy a European café." The association of
gaming, particularly *tavli*, with a non-European and internal national
habit comes to the fore here in this central issue of concealment and revelation, of the protection of an intimate sphere from the prying and judg-
mental gaze of outsiders (see Herzfeld 1997a), much like my own sensa-
tion when passing by the partially curtained gambling coffeehouse that
I described at the beginning of the Introduction.

Stephanos would prefer to sell his potential customers on the beautiful view, highlighted by the old "Venetian" lighthouse, which sits across

the water from Santrivani Square at the end of a thin promontory (the original was destroyed and the replacement was built in the late 1700s). It is a frequently photographed and represented feature of the city; looking in the opposite direction, up the aforementioned Halidon Street, provides a striking view of the craggy peaks of the White Mountains, snow-capped through much of the year. Looking to the end of the quay one can also see the fortress Frikas, where every morning at dawn a squad of Greek soldiers, after marching down to the city from the former home of Eleftherios Venizelos on the hillside east of the center of town, raises the Greek flag.

This last activity highlights the importance of Santrivani square's now somewhat occluded history in the larger story of Crete, for it memorializes the moment when the Greek flag was first raised on Cretan soil at the fortress on December 1, 1913, signifying Crete's union with Greece (Tsivis 1993, 287). Santrivani square had played a crucial role in the movement for unification; through all the long years of varied governance the square had remained a central meeting place in the town, surrounded at the turn of the century by a mixture of hotels, newsstands, coffeehouses, and restaurants (the square burned in an accidental fire in 1930). It was there that repeated demonstrations took place in the first decade of this century, calling for the union of then-autonomous Crete with Greece (Detorakis 1994, 411–15), and when the flag was finally raised at the fortress, Santri-

Chania's lighthouse, as seen from Santrivani Square in the old Venetian harbor. (Author's collection)

A view of the Venetian harbor of Chania from the lighthouse, with the White Mountains of Crete in the background. (Author's collection)

vani square was the site of the celebration. With recent (1997–99) reconstruction and renovation of the old town's cobblestone and marble alleys and streets, an octagonal space has been left in the middle of Santrivani for a new fountain; the square is evidently slowly regaining aspects of its monumental past.

This planned reconfirmation of the square's prominence is not surprising. As one of the few open places in the old town, which is dominated by narrow and twisting roads and alleys, and with its tremendous view of the mountains and the sea, the square is a natural meeting point. The square is also the local site for one of the most important holidays of the Greek calendar, Epiphany, also called the "blessing of the waters," on the sixth of January every year, when in every Greek coastal city the local principal religious official, with great ceremony, tosses a gold cross three times into the harbor. Each time young men and boys dive in the cold winter water after it, competing to be the one who will seize it and take it back to the priest. Through its mixture of contest and fortune, where a young man's ability to prevail over others becomes inextricably linked to his own religious blessing, the ceremony reveals how personal accomplishment and a trope of accountability such as religious purity come together to make sense of an outcome—in this case, why one young man obtained the cross and not another. The next day the local paper *Chania News* usually carries a brief article about the young men who retrieved the cross. Santrivani Square is thus a regular and ritual destination for Chaniots, but I learned of its prominence in turn-of-the-century Chaniot life not through discussions of Crete's drive for unification, nor through conversations I had as one among the crowd at the harbor on January sixth. Instead it was quite unexpectedly through my interest in the local history of gambling that Santrivani's history presented itself to me.

Around the end of 1995 I picked up a copy of another local paper, *Kirix* (Herald), and went to Koupes to read it. To my surprise I found a story about gambling in Chania at the turn of the century. The text was brief, reflecting the general dearth of information on early gambling in Chania, but accompanying the article was a locally famous photograph depicting a demonstration in the square in 1905, when tensions were highest between the ruling governor, Prince George (who had been appointed by the four European powers of Italy, France, Britain, and Russia after they had wrested control of the island from the declining Ottoman Empire), and a group of rebels calling for unification led by Eleftherios Venizelos. In the picture a throng of people fills the square, which was then surrounded by three-story buildings, and someone waves a large Greek flag in the crowd. (I have been told that Venizelos himself appears in the photograph, but this could not be confirmed.)

This article used the picture not for its political importance, however, but rather because it showed clearly the location of one of the most well-known gambling clubs in Chania at the time. As the article points out, on the second floor of one of the buildings was "the renowned card-playing club" of Kondilaki (Delakis 1995, 13). The juxtaposition of a significant event of national pride and the attribution of the presence, albeit invisibly, of a gambling den (there is nothing in the picture to indicate it is anything other than a coffeehouse) was a source of entertainment for most of the locals to whom I pointed out the article. "Surely, there were some playing while everyone was down in the square," one man, laughing, said to me, and this comment highlights gambling's ambivalence as both an activity contrary to collective social or national interests and one that typifies a local (and regional) self-stereotype, that of the individual gambler, beholden to no one. In this respect the position of gambling resembles that of sheep theft in the Cretan highlands, as explored by Herzfeld (1985)

This self-stereotype of Chaniots (and Cretans more generally) as crafty gamblers is not unknown elsewhere in Greece. In September 1994, the ruling conservative New Democracy party was in the midst of a scandal over wiretaps supposedly ordered by the prime minister's office. A crucial and potentially damaging witness was a retired general, Grillakis, who was believed to have overseen the phone tapping. He went into hiding immediately after the scandal broke, and it was rumored that he was holed up in a village in western Crete, near where he was born. The burning question was whether Grillakis would come forward and reveal damaging information about the New Democracy party leadership's role in the scandal. An editorial cartoon depicted Grillakis, in Cretan costume, standing on the western end of the island and saying to the party (represented by the party symbol poised in Athens on the mainland), "Be careful . . . I'm from Crete. I have aces up my sleeve!" The qualities that make a good gambler, then, are ones that make one a formidable businessperson or political player, Chaniots often claim. The photograph of Santrivani became a source of amusement not because those imagined to be playing while the political event took place outside their window were seen as ignorant or disconnected from the process but precisely *because* the qualities they exhibited over the gaming table are those that are valued in political figures. This is illustrated more directly in characterizations of Greece's political leaders by Chaniots. One Chaniot referred to Venizelos as "our best gambler" ("*o kaliteros kumartzis mas*") while adding that his greatest risk, his decision to invade Asia Minor after World War I, was also his greatest ("but only!") mistake. On several other occasions, when my interests were introduced to new acquaintances, I was asked, "Did you know that Kemal Ataturk was an excellent gambler?" or "Papandreou was tremendous [*foveros*] at cards; he was a gambler." The state, then, is another player, to be battled and against which to measure one's own position on the shifting ground of everyday experience.

Eras of Innovation and Enervation

Today, rather than being a political rallying point or location for high-profile gambling, Santrivani is a center of sociability in Chania, and as such it plays a part in the construction of a distinction between the new city above and the old town (harbor) within the Venetian walls. The old city features several churches, an old well inside a renovated house in the formerly Muslim quarter (the site of a restaurant, The Well of the Turk), two extant minarets (also in this quarter) from the era of Ottoman occupation, a charming museum in a Byzantine-era monastery, several other monasteries now the sites of private businesses, a recently renovated synagogue, and a few large mansions with multiple terraces and gardens, although these last are so crowded among the smaller buildings that their existence is not obvious. Indeed, it is not often clear in this narrow hodgepodge of stone and plaster where one building ends and another begins. The stone paving and narrow alleyways in much of the old city further contribute to this sense of distinctiveness and disorientation, winding narrowly while rising and falling to follow the hills on either side of the harbor.

The same kind of partial concealment is true for the Venetian walls that demarcate the old city. In some places they are remarkably intact. Built of many close-set stones of nearly uniform size and color, they loom high, indomitable, and not to be ignored, a deep trench that was intended to be a moat (it was never filled) running at their base. In other places, however, the walls are hidden behind rows of buildings, destroyed, or simply built over, leaving little evidence to the casual observer. Across this fickle boundary rests a central means by which Chaniots differentiate the city, distinguishing between the old city and the surrounding urban area by two terms: *limani* (harbor), to refer to the old city (although at times they use the more explicit *palia poli* [old city]), and *poli*, to refer to the surrounding city, a term most often combined with *pano*, "above" (as in *pano stin poli*, "above in the city"), as the harbor lies mostly downhill from the surrounding area. Because it falls under the purview of the archeological service, strict regulations control the appearance of the buildings in the old harbor, such that any new construction or renovation must conform to the color palette and design details that characterize the old city. This also means that there is some support (from the Greek state and the European Union, for example) available for these efforts.

To make a simple association of the old town with the past and the new areas with the present would be dangerously misleading, however. The new town is made up of buildings built for the most part since World War II, many of them in the sixties and seventies. To Chaniots, these office and apartment buildings, often four or five stories of concrete with simple large-paned windows and balconies, reflect a past era as distinctly as do the Venetian buildings around the harbor (*limani*). Although a few new businesses open regularly in the new town, such as bookstores and clothing stores, the *limani* is the site for a large amount of current capital investment in new and renovated cafés and stores, tailored both to the historical commission's requirements for their exteriors and to current trends in restaurant and store design. These businesses use custom-built furniture and comprehensive decors, reflecting the large amount of capital the owners have invested in them. An acquaintance who had recently opened a popular café in the old town despite owning a continually successful (among Chaniots) live music club "up in the city" com-

A winding alley in the old town of Chania. (Author's collection)

mented, "There isn't very much new happening in the city; everyone comes to the harbor now to relax." His café, like many others in the harbor, has a distinctive decor and theme. In this case the café is a playful throwback to thirties-era Greece, with posters and music from that time and furniture reflecting an older era; the place is also known in Chania for using an older method for making Greek coffee by heating it slowly on a bed of hot sand.[3]

The ironic result of this is that residents see the "old harbor" ("old town") as the site for "new" categories of business, as a site of innovation, whereas many shops in the city above recede into a more recent past, derided as old and ugly. This point was brought home to me by a close friend who, while we walked near the city hall in the new town, pointed to the coffeehouse on the corner, with its large-paned windows and simple furnishings, in a building that could not have been more than forty years old, and said grandly, "Here is a true, authentic, traditional *kafenio* in Chania."

The harbor is further seen as distinctive by the adoption by some of its regular residents and workers of a different form of speech specific to the harbor area, called *kolombitika* after a neighborhood on the western side of the harbor, Kolombos. This "language" is a playful alteration of Greek in which each syllable is reversed, such that *limani* (harbor) becomes, for example, *"ilamin."* The waiters at one harbor café enjoyed using *kolombitika* when visited by female friends who did not work there, whispering conspiratorially, and conspicuously, to distinguish their membership in the harbor community and common (male) interest. Such means of distinction underscore the fault lines of the social landscape, such as that between the new town and the old harbor, and further highlight the importance of concealment and revelation as a constant tension in sociability.

Whereas Santrivani lies unquestionably at the heart of the old town, no landmark better illustrates the centrality and ambiguity of the harbor versus city distinction for Chania as a whole than the central market of the city, the agora. A high, neoclassical building in the shape of a symmetrical cross, the agora was built just after Crete's unification with Greece, and, like Santrivani square, constitutes an important meeting place in Chania. Significantly, the agora sits astride the old town–new town boundary, actually built on top of the former midpoint of the Venetian fortress wall at a point where the ground on either side had become built up to its level. The primary east-west road in Chania runs in front of it on the "new" side, and across this street are the national bank, telephone company, and post office buildings, three important places for tourists and locals in Chania. The tourists change money and use the automatic teller machine at the national bank (one of few in Chania), buy stamps and mail postcards and letters from the post office, and phone home from the telephone company. Locals run errands to one or more of these buildings frequently, picking up packages at the post office, trying to get a phone line repaired or installed at the telephone company, or waiting in the interminable line at the national bank. I saw a friend of mine, a jeweler, heading up toward the agora one morning when I expected he would be just opening his store. "Where are you going?" I asked him, a bit perplexed. "Irini [his assistant] is at the store," he said, "I'll be at the bank all morning, surely. If you don't see me [at the store] by the afternoon, send someone to find me!" On the other (harbor) side, the agora's entrances open immediately onto broad, steep stairways, which lead down into the smaller streets of the old town. The sea is still a few minutes away, however, and the lack of a clear street directly to the harbor makes this route one that is used less often to reach the restaurants and cafés closer to the water than Halidon Street to Santrivani Square.

Chaniots are quietly proud of the agora, remarking on some of its practical features, if asked, noting primarily that it does not smell, like many other such markets, and that it has a lot of natural light.[4] The agora is airy and high-roofed on the inside, with renters of spaces within free to build small structures for their businesses. They include fish sellers and butchers (primarily in one "arm" of the cross), cafés, restaurants, fruit and vegetable stands, bakeries, and markets. A large newsstand sat in the middle of the cross until 1996 (it has since been relocated to a location like those of the other businesses, along one arm of the cross), and light

Chania's central market, the agora. (Author's collection)

streams in through the glass windows that run along the axes of the roof. Despite locals' comments, a smell of butcher and fish shops is strong (though not overpowering) in their quarter of the market, and the pleasant smells of bread baking and coffee brewing permeate the remaining areas. Outside, on the new side, there is a broad patio, with kiosks at either end, and boards advertising films playing at the local theaters and another one for postings of recent deaths; at least one person usually is perusing these notices somberly. Around the New Year season in 1994 a large new car appeared on this patio, the prize of a raffle run by a local neighborhood's soccer club. Tickets were 2,000 Dr each (about US$8).

Petros, the former owner of the *kafenio* described in the Introduction (a place in the newer part of town not far from city hall), opened up a new café in the agora after selling his *kafenio* to Nondas in the spring of 1995. Because space in the agora lies amid a steady stream of tourists and locals, it is in great demand, and Petros informed me that he obtained the lease on this spot through the efforts of his *koumbaros*, or marriage sponsor. The *koumbaros* usually is not a peer of the groom but rather someone older, often a friend of the family, who then becomes a patron to the man he helped marry. Petros's *koumbaros*, Yiannis, had a restau-

Inside Chania's central market (agora). (Author's collection)

rant in the agora, which gave him, as a current lessee there, an advantage
in leasing space that opened up. This he did for Petros, transferring it to
Petros's name. Petros was very excited about his new place, and told me
about his plans. "You must come see it as soon as we open," he said, "It
will be very nice, and we will sell coffee and the freshest pastries." Petros's
wife, Ioanna, was quite happy about the change in business, for there was
to be no gambling at this new place: "It's a café, not a *kafenio*," she told
me; "We will have both tourists and friends." (Her use of the term *café*
was consistent with its prevalence throughout the old town, used in the
names of many businesses, such as Koupes and Santrivani.)

For Petros, moving to the agora meant much not only in terms of increased traffic, but also in flexibility. "Look," he said, showing me around
his new place, "we could do whatever we wanted because the space is
open. At the old place it wasn't worth it to try to renovate because it was
too small and old." (Ironically, the agora is a much older building than that
which harbored Petros's *kafenio*, but that building was a postwar construction.) I asked Petros whether he thought the tourist business would
stay steady in the agora or whether more and more of them would bypass
it, heading directly to the harbor, about five minutes away. The bus stops
were the issue, for although the airport bus dropped passengers off right
in front of the agora, the bus from the overnight ferry from Athens dropped
passengers off a few blocks away at the top of Halidon Street, the one that
leads straight down to Santrivani Square. "As there are many more tourists
on the ferry than on the airplane," I asked, "will the tourists begin to pass
by the agora?" Petros assured me he understood the situation well. He told
me that he took comfort from the fact that the tourist traffic to the bank,
post office, and national telephone company building was constant. "They
will come, surely," he told me, "I know how the business will be here. We
will have to be careful in the winter [with the limited tourist and military traffic] and have success in the summer."

The similarities between this attitude and Petros's style of playing
poker were striking. Other regular players at his *kafenio* had recognized
and commented to me about (though not over the gaming table) Petros's
ability to remain steady and avoid bets of seeming desperation when his
cards were poor over several hands. Petros's expectation that the winter
was not a time to try to make money but rather a time to protect his resources until the summer matched this reputation well. Petros seemed
to find the connection obvious when I broached it in that conversation:
"Of course. They are the same, don't you know?" Indeed, in Petros's
view, this was the primary difference between his own ability to run his
old *kafenio* and that of the new owner, Nondas, who, as the vignette in

the Introduction illustrated, was having his problems that first holiday season. Nondas, Petros told me, was the same as an owner as he was as a card player, always looking to bet himself out of a losing streak. "He doesn't know how to wait, and be careful," Petros concluded. Petros's café in the agora, straddling the border between the "new" harbor and the "old" town, provided just the place for the waiting game he favored. In this way, personal characteristics, social relations, and the landscape of the city itself came together in one man's attempt to engage a notoriously capricious tourist market; for Petros and many other Chaniot gamblers the ability to navigate this shifting ground attested to their potential to succeed in any endeavor.

Dueling Pasts

Not only is there a tension in local discourse between the old and new parts of the town of Chania, but also the name of the town itself carries with it an indeterminacy that reflects Chaniots' ambivalences about their own sense of place. *Chania* is a term that denotes not only the town but also the prefecture of which it is the capital, covering the western quarter of the island and containing several distinct districts, and this dual labeling reflects the two sides of Chania's history and current Chaniot claims to a distinctive community attitude and identity, claims that often involve ongoing appeals to European affiliation as against "Eastern" elements. It is the town's history since the era of Venetian rule (1204–1669) that figures most prominently in everyday assertions about Chania's place in Crete, Greece, and Europe more generally. A continuing thorn in the side of many Chaniots is the displacement of the capital of Crete from Chania to its primary rival, Iraklion, a larger town in Crete's third prefecture (from west to east). Under Venetian rule both cities at different times served as the political center of the island, but by the end of their domination Chania had become both the mercantile and diplomatic center of Crete, with consulates from several European countries. Under Ottoman rule (1669–1898) the capital shifted again to Iraklion, and Chaniots continue to associate Irakliots with Turkish or Ottoman influence by reference to this history. As Alexandros, a pharmacist in the old harbor, put it, "The Venetians were a creative influence, the Ottomans were destructive. Look at Iraklion and you can see the difference!" When Crete became independent in 1898, Chania was again the seat of government for the island, and this continued through its unification with mainland Greece in 1913 until 1971, when the capital was shifted back to Iraklion.[5]

That this is still an important issue for Chaniots is reflected in the frequency with which I was told the local version I have related and also by the remarkable use of the Internet as an arena for this contest. The local campus of the University of Crete specializes in engineering and technical sciences, and this has resulted in a sizable number of locals—mostly students and recent graduates—who have expertise not only in using the Internet but also in designing their own Web sites. Two such sites accessed in 1996, using English for most of the text, called Chania the capital of Crete, one of them proclaiming in the title of the Web site: "Chania: The Capital of Crete!" That this battle for Cretan preeminence continues in new arenas underscores its enduring significance for even the youth of Chania. But this sore spot is but a part of the complex and at times contradictory constructions of local identity one finds in Chania. The city was regularly described to me as one of the most "European" in Greece because of its beauty, its cleanliness, the quality of its stores, and the wealth and educational level of its populace. Other cities so described were Thessaloniki and Nafplion, the three referred to as the only "cosmopolitan" cities in Greece, a claim that the Chaniots maintained was generally recognized throughout Greece. "This is not only our opinion, ask anyone!" was a familiar refrain. But Chania as a category does not easily allow the extraction of the city and its qualities from the surrounding prefecture (*nomos*), the agricultural wealth of which accounts for a large part of Chania's prosperity and the violent history of which is a large part of Chania's history as well.

Chania as prefecture invokes the mountainous region's history as a violent center of resistance to outside authority, of vendettas that last for years, of cleverness at gambling (as the story of Grillakis, the general and reluctant witness, demonstrates), and of guns and knives (the latter of which in 1992 still lined the windows of many stores near the harbor, although they had largely faded away by 2000). The spirit of mountain-centered resistance is brought into the city through its veneration of local folk heroes, such as in 1866 Square, above the harbor, where many Chaniot captains of Crete's struggles against the Ottoman empire in the 1800s are portrayed in stone, all from the waist up, aptly showing the pistol grips and knife handles at their belts.

In this portrayal, the district of Sfakia within the prefecture plays an ambiguous role. Lying on the southern coast of the island and filled with high gorges and plateaus as well as numerous secretive inlets and shores, Sfakia held out longer than any other district against foreign domination, first against the Venetians and later against the Ottoman Empire and the German occupation. Seán Damer has written about the district with re-

A knife-seller's shop in the old town of Chania. (Author's collection)

gard to the practice of drinking, but his assertion regarding the perception of Sfakians by Chaniots differs significantly from my own experience (Damer 1988). Whereas Damer asserts that in Chania, Sfakians are
"the butt of jokes by the sophisticated townspeople" (296), I found that
the meaning of the region and its people in the town is more complex.
Chaniots single out Sfakians as more everything, it seems: more "traditional," more "dangerous," more Cretan, more Greek, and more skilled
in contests of any kind, including gambling. But it would be an error to
assume these attributions are tied closely to a characteristic of "wildness" or lack of sophistication or to assume that the smiles and knowing laughter that often accompany an allusion to someone's ties to the
district are simply derisive. The local stereotype of Sfakians is that they
are skilled in any competitive pursuit, particularly business, and therefore, as in gambling, know when in business to take risks and when to
trust the status quo.

There is a dual quality to Sfakian identity here because, as one Chaniot told me, they not only were the best fighters but also were the best
merchants and politicians, using their seafaring skills and local topog-
raphy to maintain trade and other relationships of alliance with Euro-

pean powers throughout these struggles for independence. Thus in Chaniot discourse Sfakia presents a paradox: It is inhabited by people who are simultaneously both more "wild" and more "traditional," qualities often associated with "easternness" by Chaniots, yet also more "smart" and "European." This portrayal stands in sharp contrast to that of Damer, who throughout his article not only takes the statements about Sfakians by outsiders at face value alone but also interprets Sfakians' statements about themselves as narrow indices of a dated and hegemonic ideology (*palikarismos*), which, he argues, arose and continued solely on the basis of the material conditions of the region. As he writes, "The remoteness of Sfakia, and the frequent involvement of Sfakiots [*sic*] in war, have given them a characteristic independence of mind, and contempt for the State, which are still highly visible" (1988, 296). I suggest instead an approach that sees stereotypes of Sfakia, as held by both Sfakians and Chaniots alike, as negotiable aspects of rhetorical performance, invoked in various contexts, such as gambling, in various and often innovative ways. Thus, the ties to Sfakia of one dice player I knew, Andreas—a waiter at a large café on the harbor whom I had known for almost a year—were made known to me only after a particularly good night in late December 1995, when he won approximately 800,000 Dr (about US$3,200). Another dice gambler who worked at the same café told me the next day, "See? You have to watch out for the Sfakians!" alluding to Andreas's mother's father, who was from the district.

This theme of Cretan distinctiveness plays out in relations between Cretans and Greeks from other parts of the country as well. One friend related to me the story of when he was in the Greek army, serving out his required year and a half of service. Manousos told me he was surprised when the group of about seven hundred soldiers with whom he went through basic training split along regional lines, with Athenians and Cretans constituting two of the largest groups. He resented people calling him a "Cretan wild man" and their near-constant suggestions that he was unpredictable, an example of how claims to status and power (in this case, by the Athenians) can be articulated through such attributions of a lack of consistency or self-control. It is of interest to note that although, as Fabian has recognized, subordinate groups may often be identified with a lack of agency, reflexivity, or awareness of the open-endedness of time by those in power, it seems that dominant groups may also exploit the "denial of coevalness" (Fabian 1983) in an opposite manner, contrasting qualities of unpredictability and wildness on the part of others with their own sober and measured stance toward the future, in the way that Manousos's compatriots here sought to put him "in his place."

These claims about national and regional differences in degrees of self-control also find expression in Chania because of the proximity of the NATO base at Soudha Bay, a short distance out of the city. Although the base serves as a port of call for NATO ships of many different member nations, the resident military population there is dominated by U.S. marines and naval personnel, and the United States' continued heavy presence in the eastern Mediterranean (particularly in recent years) has ensured that most of the transient ships are also of the U.S. Navy. This base, the largest in the eastern Mediterranean, was the focus of much anti-American sentiment in the postjunta period (1974–79), culminating in violent protests against the base in 1978. Today this anti-American military sentiment is tempered by the year-round benefit to the city's tourist industry that both the regular visiting ships and the constant presence provide. Occasional violent but small confrontations between groups of off-duty American soldiers and locals continue, however, and I witnessed three such melees during my time in Chania. These are said always to be precipitated by disputes over women: The soldiers claim that they are attacked just for looking at a woman the wrong way; the Chaniots argue that the soldiers, drunk, grab the women as they walk along the harbor and then violently react to any attempts to assist the victim. Invariably, off-duty access for the soldiers to the city is restricted for a few days, after which a high shore patrol presence seems temporarily to prevent flare-ups. The worst results of these skirmishes were broken bones and the seemingly inevitable outcome of the Americans being thrown into the cold water of the harbor. In fact, the consistency of this result became a source of pride and amusement for many Chaniots, and any retelling of a recent such event was likely to be interrupted by eager listeners laughing and asking the only important question: "Were the Americans thrown in the harbor again?" More importantly, the proximity of the base means that Chaniots often distinguish between American visitors and those from European countries other than Greece. The Americans are ridiculed for such things as the baseball caps they are perceived as invariably wearing, which Chaniots call derisively *ta kapelakia tous* ("their little hats").

Unsettled Spaces

The tensions of ambiguity between old and new, town and prefecture, Crete and Greece, Chaniots and Americans, and Europeans or Mainland Greeks and Chaniots or Cretans, are mirrored in gambling's ambiguous position in the eyes of many Chaniots as both a sanctioned and stylish activity of the West and a secretive and seamy activity of the East. In restricting backgammon to the interior of Koupes Café—in the shadows and behind an archway through which the waiters pass—Stephanos made an equivocal statement about the place of backgammon (whether played for money, drinks, or bragging rights) in the stylish and innovative Chania of the old city and harbor. Although he did not fully forbid it, only those who were already customers were likely to see the backgammon being played as they headed to the restrooms in the back of the interior. And so it is with many of the new *stekia* (youth hangouts) in the old city, a growing destination for young Chaniots to spend their money and free time. With much thought and money devoted to furnishing a distinctive aesthetic, practices that reflect a non-European outlook may be restricted; other places—and this is critical—play up a cultural and historical element such as backgammon as yet another item and practice on which to inscribe the establishment's distinctiveness. In one such place, Khalima, the owners went so far as to have backgammon boards custom-made a jarring bright blue and orange (at quite a price) to match the color scheme. Such "historical constructivism" (Faubion 1993) is the product of a mixture of owners', designers', and customers' preferences.

These entrepreneurial manipulations of historical elements are embedded in the several longstanding and dramatic historical and geographic features visible from nearly everywhere in the old town that I have described. At another establishment, a small beerhouse (with imported beers from all over the world), very popular with a young and affluent crowd in Chania, the owner and I could play backgammon only in the early hours after opening, before many customers arrived, because the owner's wife was concerned that the place not be "like a *kafenio*." Finally, Mikrocafenio, the thirties-era place mentioned earlier, also had custom-designed *tavli* boards when it opened, made to fit in with the decor's colors and wood tones and "antiqued" to appear of the appropriate era.

If the games straddle the symbolic distinctions I have outlined, the same can be said for many of the establishments where gambling takes place, and it is on this point that I close this chapter on the tensions and ambiguities in Chania's landscape. In Chania there are café bars, some examples of which I have already discussed, many coffeehouses (*kafenia*), and *leskhes* (clubs), as well as lottery shops, homes, and converted bars, all of which may host gambling activity of one kind or another for all or certain parts of the year. This range of locations is to some extent a recent phenomenon. One of the first gamblers whom I interviewed immediately remarked that the old town had changed greatly in the last twenty years. "There were about twenty or thirty gambling coffeehouses near the harbor. Now there are only two or three down there." My own count and other interviews bore this estimate out; I located three coffeehouses with regular gambling in the old town, and only one of them was close to the actual harbor.

Coffeehouses, or *kafenia*, have long been the subject of anthropological interest in Greece. In Chania, however, this variety of establishments that I encountered was not easily subsumable under one term. Many of the places where gambling takes place, where coffee is the primary drink, where the hours of operation are the same, and where the clientele is almost exclusively male were categorized by most Chaniots consistently as coffeehouses. But mention of some of the new cafés in the old harbor elicited mixed responses.

Santé, a large café on the west side of the harbor, right on the water, was extremely popular among the youth of Chania; its customers were almost exclusively young men and women from about fourteen to twenty-two years old. Occupying two stories of an old building, with small balconies on the second floor and electronic games inside, and many backgammon boards in use at the small tables outside, Santé was in the eyes of most Chaniots the quintessential *steki*, "hangout." My friend Manolis, a young part-owner of a nightclub on the other side of the harbor, though agreeing with this, nonetheless insisted that the place was really a *kafenio*, a categorization with which some others at our table agreed. I was brought up short by the characterization, as the place seemed so different from the classic coffeehouse of the ethnographic literature. "It is a *kafenio* because people come here to have coffee, meet each other, talk, play backgammon, and pass their time," he said. It could not be a bar, in his opinion, because even though they sold alcoholic drinks, there was no loud music, no dancing, and most people bought coffee drinks (mostly "café frappés," a cold, whipped coffee drink). It could not be a taverna, he said, because there was no food, and it could not be a sweetshop because it was not for families and there were no sweets (apart from some ice cream). "What about the fact that men and women both come here?" I asked. "Women go to *kafenia* in the cities now," he told me, "It is not a big difference anyway." Although I hesitate to accept completely this characterization of coffeehouses and gender in Chania, as the men-only nature of the gambling *kafenia* described throughout this work attests, nonetheless there are other examples of *kafenia* where both men and women gather.

One such coffeehouse, and one that also presented a paradox to Chaniots in a different way, was Mikrocafeneio ("Little Kafenio"), the thirties-style café mentioned earlier. As its name, decor, and menu suggested, it was nothing other than a coffeehouse, and Chaniots alluded to it as such. But with its mixed clientele, chic popularity, and aesthetic design, it bore little resemblance to the traditional coffeehouses up in the city. Mikrocafeneio is a fascinating example of the very kind of categorical ambiguity I am interested in highlighting here because, through its self-conscious historical reference to *kafenia* of another era, it was an explicit statement about the changing nature of this important place of sociability in Greek life. Rather than a mockery or an assertion that the era of *kafenia* has passed, the Chaniots with whom I spoke about Mikrocafeneio saw it as a new and old *kafenio* simultaneously.

In a similar way, the presence or absence of gambling at any *kafenio* in Chania is an ambiguous judgment at best. With contests at the coffeehouses waged over everything from backgammon to soccer matches to card playing to where flies will land next, gambling is not an easy criterion by which to divide up establishments in Chania. Throughout this work, however, I follow the distinctions made by Chaniots themselves, and refer to some *kafenia* as "card-playing" or "gambling" *kafenia* because certain places have reputations for regularly allowing card games or dicing for substantial amounts of money. My concern is that this labeling not be construed as a general suggestion that gambling resides only at these places. After all, the two players who bet on the fly and the plates of fruit mentioned in the Introduction were, as Christoforos told me, betting large sums of money (10,000 to 20,000 Dr, or about US$50–100) at the coffeehouse where they had coffee every morning, a place without dice or even regular card playing for anything more than a few drinks.

Finally, as I mentioned earlier, the question of sociability becomes implicated with respect to gambling coffeehouses because the clientele changes frequently. Although every place has some regulars, even they play at several *kafenia,* and the reasons behind these choices mark a tension, as the quotations that open this chapter indicate, between claims to broad social ties on one hand and narrow and shameless greed on the other. In my deepest conversations with closer contacts on this issue, the explanation was a more pragmatic one that integrated both of these concerns, arguing that because the monetary stakes are so high, particularly in poker, it is not easy to spend a lot of time, apart from during the games themselves, with one's opponents. "You can, you know, become friends even with someone who lost a lot to you, but this happens rarely," noted Bobbis, a regular at Petros's (later Nondas's) *kafenio.*

It is worthwhile to note that although political affiliation has long been one of the primary influences on coffeehouse patronage, in the case of gambling *kafenia* I did not find this to be the case. This may be somewhat the effect of the lack of a strong conservative presence in Chania, which has as a whole strongly supported PASOK, the left-wing party in Greece, for some time (the fact that Chania is the hometown of right-wing New Democracy's leader Constantinos Mitsotakis notwithstanding), but I more confidently point to the sense of a clear difference, pointed out to me by Chaniots, between *kafenia* that are for everyday socializing and those that are for gambling primarily. However, as I discuss in the next chapter, class relations do inform the make-up and characterizations of some gambling locales in Chania.

In the chapters that follow instances of these kinds of links that Chaniots make between gambling arenas and everyday life include the association of business acumen with gambling ability (seen already in the case of Nondas and Petros), the mapping of tension-laden struggles that characterize gender relations and courtship onto backgammon boards and card tables in clubs, and the similarity often voiced between playing the state-sponsored lotteries and evading taxes. Chaniots make sense of gambling and gambling spaces in the town through the same distinctions by which they make sense of their city in general. Backgammon boards, small-stakes gambling for *parea* (good company), and the visibility of the games themselves become fodder for local struggles over the varied elements of Chaniot identity, encompassing everything from claims to Sfakian astuteness to accusations of cheating. It is against this backdrop that the cards and dice of the games of Chania are continually dealt and tossed, every moment a new chance to account for one's place or that of others.

Notes

1. See, for example, Herzfeld (1987, 1992, and 1997a).

2. The name of the city is pronounced "han-YAH." There are several potential ways to represent the city's name in roman script. I use "Chania" here because it is the roman form in which the name is most commonly used in commercial and municipal contexts (maps, street signs, and hotel names). A more accurate representation in phonetic terms (matching the romanization used elsewhere in this text) would be "Khania." A third form, also encountered both locally and in other contexts, is "Hania." Finally, there is an older form, "Canea," which seems to date to Venetian ownership of the island (it is the name for the city on maps from that era); this is currently seen in the names of some businesses, primarily hotels and restaurants.

3. For a fuller discussion of the uses of history, entrepreneurial risk, and the class tensions articulated through the imagined landscape of Chania, see Malaby (in press).

4. An indication of its continued significance to Chaniots is the agora's popularity as a subject in municipally sponsored graffiti by local youth artists.

5. For a comprehensive history of Crete, see Detorakis (1994). For a history of Chania, see Tsivis (1993).

2 *Things Not Being Equal*

A discussion of the divisions within the imagined landscape of Chania leads naturally to a more focused discussion of how these and other ways of construing difference manifest themselves over the gaming table. The central issue here is that of inequality, a feature of social life most obviously displayed in Chania through two discourses of difference, class and gender. Although I have more extensively treated articulations of class difference by old town entrepreneurs as they draw on an imagined landscape of the city elsewhere (Malaby in press), here I take a brief space to discuss articulations of class difference as they relate to gambling activity, in particular the locally construed differences between two different (or not so different) kinds of clubs where card playing takes place. I then turn to an examination of backgammon (*tavli*), where its comparatively public exposure of two players' differences in position (on the table and, by extension, beyond it) provides for an appropriate exploration of how tropes of accountability are used, verbally and nonverbally, in public constructions of hierarchy. In the case of backgammon, the tropes are luck and skill, and they are both contrasted and combined creatively by backgammon players over the course of the game. Throughout and after this discussion, I also consider how constructions of gender difference manifest themselves in two of the primary sites where these inequalities appear, both publicly and among circumscribed groups: cafés (where the game is backgammon) and card-playing clubs. In both of these spaces women and men play together, unlike in the other forms of gambling I explore in this work. The mapping of hierarchies over the gaming table, as is evident in the case of backgammon, is seen by Chaniots as mirroring (and also constituting) the ongoing struggle for social position in everyday life. This manifests itself in both continuing instances of class-articulated tension and in the endeavors involved in courtship and kin relations (particularly among Chania's youth).

It is worthwhile to note that this chapter also gives me an opportunity to engage the issue of how gambling practice relates to the performance of manhood in Chania. Although the reader will no doubt note that this issue runs throughout this work, it is foregrounded here because the ethnographic material is more amenable to a discussion of a topic that bears directly on questions of power and inequality. Gambling and manhood is not the primary focus of this text as a whole, however. The relationship between performance and manhood in the Cretan context already been treated masterfully by Herzfeld (1985, 1991, 1997b), and I am concerned here with a different aspect of social performance: how through it actors engage the unpredictability of experience. Although some of the modes of this engagement are deeply shaped by ideals of gender identity as it is constructed in the Cretan context, the engagement of chance is not reducible to them, and although I seek to note the influence of gender identity on such action where relevant, my broader aim is to provide a clearer sense of how social analysts might go about understanding such encounters with the uncertain wherever they appear.

Clubs of Contest

In many ways similar to older coffeehouses, such as those described in chapter 1, are the card clubs, which have similar decor and also have separate areas for sitting and playing. They are called *leskhes,* meaning "clubs," although the membership at these places is not closed. But although similarities with the gambling *kafenia* are many, there are several crucial differences between them. First, *leskhes* have significantly different hours of operation from *kafenia.* Whereas coffeehouses, even those with gambling, often close by 11 P.M., the *leskhes* only begin to have games around 10 in the evening, and they continue until 4 or even 5 A.M. Also, the players at *leskhes* generally prefer games such as *thanasis* or *berimba,* games based more on chance distributions of cards than, for example, poker, and they play them for lower stakes per hand than poker (although because they play for more hours in a night, the difference in stakes over a given evening is less marked).[1] Finally, and perhaps most importantly, women and men play together at *leskhes,* a fact that was surprising given the other similarities with coffeehouses. The women often are widows, or they are married and play with or without their husbands on any given night.

On a related point, the clientele at *leskhes* also does not vary to nearly the same degree as at gambling *kafenia*. Sotiris, an owner of a card club in Chania, explained that the people who play in *leskhes* love cards, not money, so the stakes are a little lower and the games less antagonistic, a claim that underscores the locally contested meaning of gambling. Sotiris's assertion that gambling at *leskhes* (in contrast to that at *kafenia*) does not run counter to sociability was not accepted by regular customers at Petros's (later Nondas's) *kafenio*. They recognized that *leskhes* players were less interested in games emphasizing direct competition, such as in poker, but saw in that preference only more evidence of their unmediated interest in making money without having to engage in the difficult psychological reading that marks a good poker player. These construals of difference between players of different kinds of games (and frequenters of different kinds of gambling spaces) also reflects the difference in ages of the clientele: Gambling *kafenia* tend to have middle-aged men still working, whereas the patrons of *leskhes* often are retired or nearing retirement. Also, accusations of cheating were more common at the *leskhes* I observed than at the gambling coffeehouses, and it seems that the presence of married couples there precipitates these confrontations because they are often accused of exchanging prearranged signals. This, too, suggests that Sotiris's benign appraisal of the relationship between *leskhes* and sociability is a strategic representation.

In one case of such cheating, Sotiris, the owner, and his wife, Eleni, were playing *berimba* against another couple. Yiannis, a regular who had introduced me to the club, then came in, and Eleni got up to make him coffee while the cards were reshuffled for the next hand. The woman of the other couple, Neni, then began to comment on how badly it was going for her and her husband, and after a moment she looked at the score sheet. This seemed to make her more upset, and soon she was standing up and arguing with Sotiris; it was a one-sided argument, however, for Sotiris said little, while Neni continually asked sarcastic questions about how Sotiris knew when to play one card or another. Before I knew it she was getting her coat from the rack behind her and telling her husband, Pavlos, still seated, that they were going because "They're eating us" (*"mas trone"*), an expression that is invoked not only to comment on an indisputable defeat but also to imply that some underhanded means were used by the winners.[2] It was still quite early in the evening, only about 11 o'clock (often *berimba* was played early in the evening until full tables of *thana-*

sis, for which they preferred to have at least five players, could be formed), and silence fell over the room. As they began to walk out, Eleni, who had been busy making coffee, looked up and noticed, and said, somewhat confused (and a little concerned), "You're leaving?" After they left, Eleni moved to sit in her place and said, "She is the absolute worst." No one contradicted her, but no one agreed either. Meanwhile, Sotiris and Yiannis were discussing the situation, and later Yiannis told me that the couple was upset because they thought Sotiris and his wife were cheating. "Were they?" I asked. "Who knows?" Yiannis replied, "But you should know that whenever Neni loses, it's not her fault." Here a performative failure on Neni's part led to social disapprobation, as her continual reliance on tropes that deflect responsibility seemed to have jeopardized her credibility with other players.

The term *leskhi* can also refer to private clubs with closed memberships, where gambling also takes place—there are two of these in Chania—and the dual use of the term reflects ongoing tension in the city's card-playing community. The private clubs have as members local professionals—pharmacists, doctors, and lawyers—whereas those who play at the *leskhes* are, though sometimes wealthy, nonetheless of middle-class backgrounds, either in the tourist industry or another business. The class tension this distinction reveals was made evident to me when after numerous attempts I was able to gain entry into one of the city's two private clubs. I relate the evening here at length because of the numerous ways in which it highlights the ambiguous place of gambling amid local struggles over class, European-ness, and other axes of identity.

My contact, Markos, a pharmacist, was a man with whom I had spoken only on the phone; I had made contact with him only through the efforts of a fellow pharmacist whom I knew in the old town. Markos had stood me up on two previous occasions at the club, leaving me calling from a nearby kiosk to locate him. On the evening he finally showed I arrived at the club about 8:15 P.M. and waited just a minute or two before Markos arrived. His manner as he walked up to me was noticeably reserved and a little agitated, although polite enough. He took my arm and led me over to a small leather couch that rested against the wall just inside the door to the club before a second door; we were quite noticeably within, yet not within, the confines of the club itself. We sat, and he turned to me and said, though kindly, "What do you want here?" I immediately sensed that there might be a problem and that the reasons for his two previous cancellations may have been more than the "pharmaceutical emergencies" he had claimed. At my pause, he elaborated that he asked because he did not think that there was anything of interest for me there. He went on to describe the club as different from the "other *leskhes*" I may have seen. The people here, he said, are educated (*morfomeni*), and very different from those who play in "the clubs that you can see from the street," a revealing comment, as it underscores the role of visibility in claims to legitimacy. I replied that I was interested not just in gambling for a lot of money but in games in general, to understand the social role that games can play in culture. This seemed to ease his concerns somewhat, and he soon invited me to follow him to the back to sit, "drink something," and talk.

The *leskhi* occupied the first and basement floors of an apartment building. The building's mid-1960s style was evident in the polished blonde oak beams across the ceiling, the smooth-lined bar and shelves behind of similar wood, the front coatcheck desk of the same wood, the smoked-glass lamp fixtures, the 1960s-style large speakers mounted on the walls, and the high-ceilinged, accent-free, white-painted structure of the rooms as a whole. By contrast, the curtains (always closed) were velvet and a reddish color, complete with tiebacks of gold braid, so imposing that they were the first thing I noticed when I entered the room. The floor was covered with a number of intricately colored carpets, the chairs were heavy and either plush or leather-covered, and the small tables were marble-topped. Running to the back was a hall along which were rooms, probably two or three, with three or four doors opening into them, where the members played cards. As we walked, Markos whispered to me, again a little nervously, that I should not say why I was there to anyone we met.

We sat in one of the rooms in back, a room with two entrances. In it there were three occupied tables: One of them had a group of only women, five of them, playing; another table, near us, had three women and one man, and they were playing *berimba*; the final table had two couples, and they also were playing *berimba*. The people in this back room seemed to be between the ages of fifty and sixty.

We spoke about the *leskhi* itself for a little while. He told me that it was a very old *leskhi*, more than 100 years, he said, and that they used to have an old building next door, a beautiful building, but they had been obliged to move from it because maintaining it was too expensive. Now, they all rent the current location, he said. In 1995 there were 130 members, all male (although their wives can attend the *leskhi*, even without their husbands), and a new member must have the approval (by secret ballot) of 75 percent of the membership. There is no specific rule about level of education, but every member, he said, must be *morfomenos*.

We spoke briefly about casinos, and he seemed disdainful of them: "Only the casino wins," he said. We spoke further, and I asked him about the state games and he gave the same opinion, that only the state wins in that kind of gambling. However, shortly it came out that the previous year eighty of the members took a trip together, that the *leskhi* organized, to Kerkira (Corfu) to gamble at the casino there. We returned to the subject of the *leskhi* itself, and he again stressed that gambling itself is not central there. It is, he said, "only for company" (*parea*). He called the *leskhi* "a family place," and therefore not like "lower places." The *leskhes* that are just for gambling are "totally different," he reiterated.

Noting the couples at two of the other tables, I asked whether husbands and wives played together often. He said that disagreements often arose when a husband and wife played together as a team, reflecting, I thought, at least one similarity with the "lower" leskhes. When, after his insistence that the gambling there was not the point, I compared their playing for "small stakes" to the playing for drinks in the villages, he immediately seized on the analogy. "Yes, exactly," he said, "it's like in the villages." He then spoke a bit about the level of stakes at the *leskhi*. "We don't play for much money," he said, "A person cannot lose more than, say, one thousand drachmas in one night playing here." I was immediately skeptical of this claim; the nearby couples were playing *berimba* for 10 Dr a point, which meant that a 2,000-point difference in score (common at the end of the game) would result in the losing side's owing 20,000 Dr (about US$90). Over the course of an evening, in which one could play six or seven such games, the stakes would certainly be substantial. (Also, when I related this story to others in Chania, most of them expressed disdainful disbelief, saying with conspiratorial confidence that they played for a lot of money at this *leskhi*.)

The distancing of the two kinds of *leskhes* from each other is mutual, as an owner of another "lower" *leskhi*, Christoforos, made clear to me (this was the same gambler who told the story of betting on a fly and plates of fruit). Christoforos's *leskhi* was near the center of Chania and enjoyed a steady business year-round, making it one of the most well-known gambling locations in town. It turns out that the president of the other private club, which shared many members with the first one, was Christoforos's godfather. Christoforos then characterized the gambling at the private club I had visited. "They are all dirty" (*vromiki*) he said. "Ten percent of them are clever, and they steal money from the other ninety percent. They won't let me in because they don't want another clever person in the club." It is clear that his personal experience shaped his view of the club, which he saw as filled mostly with passive victims of a few clever members, a rather scathing portrayal. Others in Chania saw the exchange differently and suggested that Christoforos's expectation that his godfather's membership would ensure him one as well was completely unreasonable. "He's not their type. What is he thinking?" a gambler who played regularly at Christoforos's *leskhi* remarked. The lines of contest over gambling and the signs of class membership are bitterly drawn, and again the question of visibility, of protecting space from the hazardous scrutiny of others, runs throughout this dispute. Christoforos's comments suggest that the "ninety percent" who lack the cleverness of the minority are their victims because of their own lack of knowledge about what is happening around them. This theme of constructing difference over the ability to recognize and understand one's circumstances is perhaps even more fundamental to competition over the backgammon table.

The Din of Inequity

Because it is a practice central to Greek national conceptions of game-playing skill and competitiveness, backgammon is not always played for material stakes in Chania, but the fact that individual (and sometimes national, as when Chaniots played foreigners such as me) status is so vividly at stake in any given game makes backgammon just as much a form of gambling in the sense with which I am concerned here. Through its clear framing of two combatants within a local and (to some degree) public social field and its continuously intriguing mix of chance and skill in its three forms, *tavli* highlights three ideas that are present in all Chaniot gambling: style, chance, and contest.

Tavli often becomes a continuous subtext to friendships and other more casual but regular interactions. One close contact of mine, Nikos, who ran a hotel that he and his brothers owned, during the quiet part of the afternoon during the off-season would call over the owner of a souvlaki stand across the street, who he knew would also not be busy, to play a few games of *tavli* and add yet another chapter to a long history of games between them, with the winner gaining a certain smile and saunter, at least until the next round. Even the loser might find some recompense in retelling a particularly remarkable game, where one side may have escaped from a seemingly impossible situation, going on either to win gloriously or lose tragically. In *tavli* individual style and a discursively elaborated tension between luck and skill become the repertoire of players' confrontations not simply with each other, but with the game's unpredictability itself, where indeterminacy arises not simply from the dice rolls but also from other sources, both social and performative. In the unfolding game, the inequities (of position on the board, of luck with the dice, of style in playing, of the score, and of skill at the game itself) become more and more apparent to any spectators, and the players themselves attempt to shape those understandings through often grandiose gestures and claims.

Tavli is a much more publicly visible game in Chania than the others I found in the city. Even state gambling takes place most often in the relative social and physical isolation of the lottery shop (*lahiopraktorio*) and is nearly always a singular activity (see chapter 4). And whereas poker is a game of near silence punctuated by periodic bursts of volubility, backgammon is a game of continuous sounds, both from the game board and from the players themselves. *Zaria* (dicing), though played in a sizable group, is almost always resolutely hidden from public view for reasons of protection from the authorities and hazardous gossip. As *tavli* is played in cafés and *kafenia* (and outside them in good and bad weather), the sounds of dice clattering and pieces clacking overlaid with the exhortations and exclamations of the players (directed just as often at the dice as at the opponent) are never far in Chania. Crescendos are all the more likely upon the arrival of a particularly helpful roll to one player, who then matches the volume of his piece slamming by the intensity of his exclamations of triumph. In many ways in backgammon sound thus becomes the most immediately evident marker of hierarchy, albeit of a temporary kind. But this foregrounding of noise is misleading and constitutes perhaps the most dangerous trap for a player of the game, who may begin to pay too much attention to an opponent's boisterous performance and not enough to what is happening on the board.

It is this quality of the game that makes it a particularly appealing metaphor for the uncomfortable social interactions where strangers meet, such as when, as a longtime Chaniot master of the game told me, the two families of a couple planning to marry meet for the first time (the *proxenio*). Such encounters, Chaniots assert, raise the level of attention paid to the details of others' behavior; in a way that also echoes the reading of others in poker (see chapter 3), the smallest gesture can become a decisive indicator of attitude. Given *tavli*'s more public place as compared with poker, however, it would be fair to say that skill at *tavli* is not so much about the skill of reading others that poker demands as about the skill of self-presentation, or social performance when many eyes, not only your opponent's, may be on you. This feature of gambling also gives mileage to attempts to map gender difference onto it. The ability to perform publicly, in ways that distract one's opponent, while not losing sight of the "real" circumstances and the best ways to make use of what chance provides is strongly identified in Chania with concepts of Cretan maleness. In this respect men and women can make use of backgammon's briefly constructed hierarchies in the pursuit of their interests, particularly in the area of courtship.

Backgammon's public aspect might at first appear at odds with the concerns of business owners, such as Koupes's Stephanos, who seek to regulate its appearance in their establishments. Yet such instances of cultural intimacy, as Herzfeld has argued, exemplify the "aspects of a cultural identity that are considered a source of external embarrassment but that nevertheless provide insiders with their assurance of common sociality" (Herzfeld 1997a, 3). I add that in the case of backgammon it is not only a mode of common sociality for Chaniots (and for Greeks, generally) but a common practice and metaphor for the establishment of hierarchy, however temporary. Demanding as it does elements common to success in everyday life and in the game itself (luck, strategy, and boisterous performance), backgammon is nonetheless (or therefore) also a source of potential embarrassment, as the misdirection of grandiose and loud gestures and declarations for the purposes of winning the game risk being misunderstood by cultural outsiders as indicators of an imagined (as "wild," "traditional," or "irrational") Cretan personality. This ambivalence over the game's place in Chaniot life also appears in discussions of its status as a form of gambling.

Although the game is often played for drinks, nearly all the Chaniots with whom I spoke did not immediately classify *tavli* as gambling. "Sometimes there may be five thousand drachmas under the board, and that is [significant] money, but not often," one man said to me, illustrating the practice by pretending to slide money under an imaginary board as we watched a heated contest between two old foes at Koupes (inside, of course) on the harbor. This hesitancy to group *tavli* with *zaria* and card playing (for money) is linked to the distinction between the terms *koumari* and *tsogos*. Both can be glossed as "gambling," but whereas *tsogos* has a more formal aspect (such that any bet, however small, qualifies), *koumari* points specifically to a high-stakes, illicit, and to-be-hidden kind of gambling, epitomized by dice gambling. Upon discussion about whether *tavli*, if played for drinks or money, fit the category of *tsogos*, nearly all my informants agreed that, in this respect, it was gambling. It was the potential association of *tavli* with the secretive and morally suspect *koumari* that prompted this categorical defensiveness.[3]

Thus, *tavli*, unlike any other game that I encountered in Chania, is talked about and presented in the media as occupying a special role in the daily life of Chaniots and Greeks more generally. Numerous national newspaper articles discuss its broad appeal across generations throughout Greece, and although I could locate no recent books on card games in Greece, *tavli* was the subject of several. One of these was exemplary in its presentation of the rules and strategy of *tavli* on one hand and its place in Greek life generally on the other, even dividing these discussions into two volumes. In addition to regarding *tavli* as characterized by a changing balance of skill and luck, a view consistent with my research, the first volume discusses *tavli*'s position in Greek popular culture and sees two qualities as fundamental to understanding it: beauty (*omorfia*) and worth, or value (*axia*) (Maltezopoulou 1982). This portrayal by implication distinguishes *tavli* from other games as played in Greece, and this is of interest given *tavli*'s dual status (in the cultural intimacy sense) as something to be forbidden from Western view (as at Stephanos's café) and something to celebrate as a hallmark of Greek national identity. It is not clear to what extent paeans to the game in such texts both respond to and constitute this association, but in Maltezopoulou's presentation the game's beauty is found in its balance of luck and skill, which in his view creates continual fascination for its players, and its worth lies in its "pure" pitting of two opponents against each other in an open and fair arena. As I discuss here, however, more than any other game tavli invites the scrutiny of nonparticipants, so to see it as exemplary of an isolated head-to-head contest is misleading. Without money on the table, social standing and (particularly when Greeks play non-Greeks) national pride are at stake, and the presentation of oneself as having and exploiting the upper hand is highly valued, if done well. The ability to engage performative indeterminacy, then, is most tested in *tavli*, with biting penalties from strangers and acquaintances for inept social performance.

A consideration of the context of the game leads directly to the issue of *tavli*'s place in Chaniot sociability. That *tavli* should be so dramatically opposed to *koumari* in Chaniot discourse is an indication of the intimate link between the game and sociability as well as national and individual pride. *Tavli* is distinguished from all of the other forms of gambling I describe here (with the possible exception of state gambling, which is for the most part an individual activity) by the fact that, as far as I was able to observe, the game was never played between complete strangers. In poker and *zaria*, by contrast, one must have some contact or entry into the place where the game takes place, but it is entirely possible if not common for two of the players in these groups not to have met. The most obvious reason for this difference is that *tavli* is for only two people, and thus its restricted conventions of participation are an indication of the social intimacy that head-to-head competition over a common board entails. In every game I witnessed or played, the two opponents had already developed an acquaintance of some kind, either through patronage of the same café or *kafenio* and social contact that ensued, through working together (such as at Koupes, where the waiters played *tavli* whenever business was slow), or through a mutual acquaintance, who may relinquish his place at the board to a just-arriving friend so that the newcomer may meet and play his current opponent.

Because *tavli* is played so commonly in Chania, nearly every café and *kafenio* has boards available for customer use. One striking feature of *tavli* is its popularity among all generations in Chania. Unlike cards, which one sees the youth of Chania play only rarely, at their *stekia* (hangouts, often café-like businesses) tavli is everywhere and becomes a forum for contests and contact between men and women as well as a way for friends of the same sex to pass the time. One middle-aged woman in Chania, who ran a large hotel, contended that *tavli*'s popularity was out of control. "It's a mania," she said, "they play it everywhere," and this sentiment echoes the concern over the exposure of the game, and Chaniots' passion for it, to outsiders, as in the actions of Koupes's owner.

My first encounter with the level of intensity that a *tavli* contest can kindle for Chaniots came at the first gambling *kafenio* to which I was able to gain entry. Arriving one evening to meet a friend of a friend (as such anthropological attempts at entry into bounded spaces so often begin) I entered what was to be the first of many gambling *kafenia*, although at the time I struggled to take in its myriad features. This particular place, Ftelia, was well known in Chania, having been around since the late 1950s and situated on a broad street in an upper-middle-class part of town.[4] Other gamblers in Chania never failed to recognize the place if I brought it up, and it was often listed or mentioned by them to me in more general discussions of gambling in Chania. Its reputation was that it had high-stakes gambling, with poker and *thanasis* played in nearly equal amounts. Its customers, most of them between forty and sixty-five years of age, reflected the surrounding upper-middle-class neighborhood in which nearly all of them lived, including many shop owners and bank administrators. Ftelia was in an older building, with a large veranda and front room—a building that looked somewhat out of place amidst the apartment buildings along the tree-lined street. The veranda was rarely used from fall to spring, and never for gambling. Thus, the empty and pushed-aside tables and chairs on it, along with the lush potted plants blocking the windows along the back of the veranda, made the actual inside of the *kafenio* seem even further removed from the street and its prying eyes.

Inside, the *kafenio* was split, like many card-playing *kafenia*, into two sections, divided by a small rail from front to back, the left-hand tables for higher-stakes games and lower-stakes games on the right. Both sections had four or five round card-playing tables and a couple of smaller two-person tables. The night I first arrived there were about thirty men in the *kafenio,* some playing *thanasis* on the left and others playing solitaire, reading newspapers (those aligned with the political right, such as *Eleftheros Tipos*), and talking. The walls had many pictures and posters of women, taken from calendars and advertisements, their presence underscoring the maleness of the environment.

While I was taking all of this in, my friend Kostas tapped my elbow and pointed toward a small table in the left section, where two players were audibly playing *tavli.* "Let's go watch," Kostas said, and we soon found chairs near the contest. The two players were at a small rectangular table, one common in *kafenia* and the perfect size for an open backgammon board, leaving just enough room on the ends for the players' coffee and cigarettes. As is the norm in Chania, they played three different forms of backgammon, playing one game of each and then repeating the set again as necessary (these forms are described later in this chapter).

On this night at Ftelia, one of the players seemed to be quite lucky with his rolls from very early on, getting many doubles and winning the first two games very quickly. As his streak of good luck increased, he became more and more gestural and vocal, exclaiming "Come on!" (*"Ela!"*) as he threw the dice dramatically with a sudden motion, which caused him to send at least one of the dice skittering off the board and across the floor several times. He also loudly slapped down each of the pieces as he played, again talking as he did so. It is worthwhile to note that, with good fortune evidently on his side, the player's actions stood in marked contrast to those of a player in similar straits at a poker table. There, one enjoying a run of luck would seek not to change anything, instead trying to constrain one's actions, hoping not to disturb whatever ultimately unknowable factors accounts for the current good fortune. The reason for this contrast has to do with the relationships between luck, skill, visibility, and knowledge (of the layout of pieces on the board, primarily), and it is in this way that *tavli* opens the door for dramatic enactions of hierarchy.

The most dramatically audible element of this performance of one's dominance is the technique of slapping down *tavli* pieces with great volume and authority. It is a practice so common and yet so remarkable to one unfamiliar with it—and quite difficult for a novice to attempt—that it demands a description here. In a swift motion the player raises a hand above and then lowers it, palm down, toward the *tavli* surface, with the piece held between the thumb and the tips of the fingers. Upon descending, however, the thumb is removed, and the player drops the hand faster than gravity can pull the piece down, the piece staying against the fingertips, almost seeming visibly to levitate if the gesture is large and deliberate enough. With a volume born of the necessary speed gained on its descent, the piece slams full onto the board with a resounding *clack.* The trick is to accomplish this feat against gravity with either a repeated casualness, such that nearly every move entails a slight slap of this kind onto the board (and thereby implying that every move this player makes is worthy of attention), or to do it with a dramatic and controlled tempo at particularly significant moments, the piece seeming to defy physics for the briefest of moments; many players use both techniques to varying degrees. Nikos, a young waiter at Koupes café, for example, from the very beginning of a match slapped down all of his pieces, on every move, but he did not follow this style when playing opponents against whom he had competed many times. I asked him why in such cases he slapped pieces only at significant moments in the game and he said, "They know me; I cannot make them fear me!" Indeed, slapping every piece down is common when two people play for the very first time, and serves as an initial foray into learning whether one's opponent will be distracted by such performance over the course of the game.

In the case of either style, the significance of the gesture underscores moves that are particularly devastating to one's opponent's chances, but they also illustrate the player's ability to dominate the physical surroundings and, it seems, even the physical laws governing them. The suggestion is, furthermore, that the player's embodied skill over the pieces renders the play of chance in the game secondary, a claim that becomes even more clear in the common practice of calling one's rolls, discussed later. This tension between skill and chance appears again and again in this game.

It is because of the prevalence of such manipulation of the board and its pieces that Chaniots can become quite particular about the characteristics of good *tavli* boards. Ones that are covered in leather or vinyl, with a soft lining, were rejected by every person with whom the subject came up, and a friend who had owned a small convenience store complained to me how he was stuck with about twenty such boards after he, expecting the preferred all-wood form, received them from a supplier. Wooden boards not only provide a solid surface for the rolling of the dice and slapping of the pieces but also come in a wide variety of sizes, with the larger preferred, and the pieces preferably are made out of something more dense than the most common plastic, which most players found too light: "This is not a real *tavli* piece," one man said to me. "Look, it has no weight, it won't stay in place [on the board]."

There is also a range of distinctive styles and strategies available for those who seek to gain the upper hand through misdirection. It was at the *steki* with the garish blue-orange backgammon boards that I encountered the most striking style of *tavli* play on the part of a young man who was an acquaintance of Nikos, a regular opponent of mine. Having won a series of games with Nikos, I was enjoying a cup of coffee at his expense when Christos walked through the room, saw Nikos, and stopped to shake his hand and say hello. Nikos introduced us and said, "You must play him," getting up as he said this to allow and encourage Christos to sit down opposite me. We began to play, and I quickly realized the source of the mischievous glimmer in Nikos's eyes as he had suggested that we play. Christos played backgammon as a magician manipulates a deck of cards or a set of overturned cups. His hands moved fluidly across the board, at times dipping nearly imperceptibly to move a piece, which he also did in unusual ways. For example, if he had two pieces side by side and wanted to move one behind the other two spaces forward, he did not "jump" the front one with this piece, as one would conventionally do. Instead, he slid *both* pieces forward a station, which in the end accomplished the same thing by making the pieces "trade places" (with the former back piece now slid forward to represent the piece that did not move and the former front piece pushed ahead one space to represent the back piece ahead two spaces). This kind of technique, which Christos used in many different situations in subtly different ways, dazzled the eye and mind, and getting used to it took a fair amount of time.

Because we played the game at a regular pace, and I realized that I could not in that tempo always determine whether Christos had played correctly or not, I felt more and more disconcerted. In raising the level of skill needed to oversee the validity of his moves while doing nothing in his technique or moves against the rules of the game, Christos emphasized and exploited the indeterminacy of *tavli*, one of a performative kind, in which one tries to monitor the board and guard against the other player's "mistakes" amid a turmoil of sound and gesture. When I asked why he played this way, he shrugged and replied simply, "To make it interesting."

Certainly in *tavli* the body occupies a central role, as both Christos's play and the slapping technique make clear. In rolling the dice, players also use many different such embodied techniques, often exaggerated for a particularly important roll. These styles match to some degree those used in dice gambling (see chapter 5), with some players throwing the dice up onto the board as their hand drops below the edge of the table, a technique that seems to defy physical laws much as the slapping technique does, and with somewhat the same purpose: to draw attention to a particular moment and its outcome, where a "mistake" on the player's part (a die bounces on the table and skitters across the floor; a piece hits the board at an odd angle and jumbles pieces around it) evokes playful jibing or outright derision. The body is further implicated in the regulation of game tempo, such as in the prevalent practice of snatching the dice up as soon as the other player has thrown them. This habit readies the dice for one's throw, which can then be done as soon as the other player has committed to a particular action (always itself a matter of individual judgment). The game can move quite quickly as a result, particularly toward the end if both players are removing pieces simultaneously. At this point, the play of the results is so standardized that strategic decisions become few and far between, leaving each player to grab the dice and roll just shortly after they stop moving, as, for example, at the end of the game at Ftelia described earlier. During the middle of the game this can be a source of some confusion and breaks in tempo, however, as a player may ask to see the dice result if they were seized too quickly for a glimpse of the numbers.

A few players I knew exploited this kind of attention to the dice to signal an illegal move on their opponents' part, arising most often through a miscounting of the spaces. In this practice, rather than calling verbal attention to the error, the opposing player throws *one die*, which, with the other player watching intently for the result, leads most often to a stuttered pause and then a questioning glance from the other player, who, missing the second die, looks to see what happened. Only after a moment does it sink in that a mistake was made, and the player looks over his or her previous move to see what went wrong, resolving it sometimes, other times requiring an abrupt comment or gesture by the roller toward the offending piece.

The risk of exposure here, then, may usefully be described as entailing the domain of performative indeterminacy, in contrast to poker, where the revelation and discernment of intents and resources, entailing questions of social indeterminacy, are more at issue. Instead, in backgammon the danger is to be exposed as one inattentive or unskilled at the game or unable to give meaning to one's moves through meaningful, if difficult to execute, gestures, such as the slapping of the pieces or the unusual tossing of the dice. Tied as *tavli* is, albeit ambivalently, to ideas of national and gender identity by Chaniots, the stakes of appearing incompetent become all the more pointed.

To return to the game between the players at Ftelia, the other player, who was clearly losing the game, also slapped down his pieces, but less audibly, and he spoke quite a bit less. Staring at the board, the smoke from a cigarette in his hand curling above, he continually told the other player, "Play!" ("*Peze!*")[5] and became increasingly motionless and severe in tone as his losing continued. In the third game, however, things were not so clear. The game was much closer this time and attracted a few more spectators (three or four), and here the conversation over the game became somewhat muted, both players focusing on the game and playing it with a regular and swift tempo, as if with the outcome in doubt they were doubly eager to see who would win. The first player won in the end, but the next game it seemed that the first player's streak had truly left him, and he became increasingly frustrated, cursing when the dice brought a particularly unfavorable result ("Screw it!" "*Gamo to!*"). The second player's mood visibly improved, and now it was his turn to become more vocal and gestural, calling to the group of onlookers with every positive roll, "Look at what happened there!" and "Now it's going well!" He won this game quickly, and as it was winding down and this outcome became clear, the first player, despite the fact that he was ahead by two games (one upon his impending loss), finally threw his pieces across the table and stood up, acknowledging the shift of fortune away from him.

Although this event occurred between two players I did not come to know well, it is such a clear example of practices I encountered again and again with other contacts that I present it here. I also hope by this means to make a central point about *tavli* as played in Chania. Unlike the other games I discuss here, *tavli* is a frequently visible game, such that spectators often are able to follow a string of games even when they do not know the participants. This exposure of the contest to unknown but potentially damaging public appraisal, the central risk of *tavli*, raises the stakes of the contest for the participants. *Tavli* therefore is a common currency for onlookers and players, an arena of contest where one's moves, one's ability to see the board, one's evident luck or skill, and one's engagement of these uncertainties in the context of a broader social one underscore the contest not only between players over the table but between the player (or players) and the peripheral field of eyes and ears following the match.

In this respect, *tavli* is an illuminating example of the dangers inherent in a simple application of a public versus private dichotomy to everyday experience in Chania. In this case, the conventions of the game require that the opponents know each other, and this condition plus the common participation in the play over the common board establishes a level of spatial and social intimacy, confining to a certain extent relevant action to the space between the players. But *tavli* is also the most public of games, and this intimate contest is never fully separated from public inspection. It is this tension between the (not so) private displays between the players, with the references to past contests that often emerge in them, and the threat of potentially rewarding or detrimental local appraisal that makes the absence of money incidental to *tavli*'s status as a game involving a high amount of risk and substantial social stakes.

Formal Questions

Like the other games I address throughout this work, I contend that some structural features of *tavli* shape how players construe the patterns of outcomes as the game proceeds. The goal of *tavli* in all its forms is the same: to move one's fifteen pieces in a U-shaped direction (in a direction opposite from one's opponent) along twenty-four triangular stations into one quarter of the board (different for each player) from which one removes them with appropriate dice rolls until the player doing so first wins the game. When we sat down to watch the game at Ftelia they were playing *fevga* (from the Greek verb *fevgo*, meaning "to leave"), a form that casual and regular players in Chania characterized to me without exception as the one involving the most strategy and skill, with the chance of the dice playing a lesser, though still significant, role. This is because in *fevga* a single piece can block a station from use by an opponent, and it takes a high degree of skill to build strings of six single pieces in a row, blocking one's opponent from further progress around the board. The subsequent difficulty one has in moving, of "leaving," one's home side of the board when so blocked, and the importance of timing in the blocker's own decision to stop blocking and leave for the other ending area, both account for the name of the game. "It is the queen of *tavli* games," a friend explained, "because there is so much strategy."

In another form, *plakoto,* single pieces can be frozen in place by an opponent's, which provides a welcome opportunity to slam one's piece down on the table as I described earlier, making as much sound as possible (the name *plakoto* is fittingly derived from the verb *plakono,* meaning "to fall down upon" or "to bury under"; the related word *plaka* can mean "gravestone") before finally and deliberately sliding it into exact position "on top" of (though literally next to on the triangular station) the now impotent piece. The sexual imagery is apt, obvious, and often commented on by the players (such as through the use of the verb *khtipao,* "to strike," a common metaphor for the man's role in intercourse [see also

Herzfeld 1985, 159]). The open piece or *poúli* (with the accent on the first syllable), vulnerable to such immobilization, often is called a *poulí* (with the accent on the second syllable), meaning "bird," and the clever play on words here transforms the "piece" into a object easily taken—a "sitting duck," as it were.[6] This transformation is also tied to the use of *poulí* to describe women, the term associating them with the same vulnerability to male conquest. It was while playing *plakoto*, then, that Yiannis had the most opportunities to "fall down upon" one of Kostas's pieces, before which he would refer to the vulnerable piece, saying, "You left me a *poulí* [piece or "chick"] to take, eh?" (In another story that I relate later in this chapter, these meanings were deployed by two young men competing over a woman's affections.)

Plakoto is seen as having a nearly equal mixture of luck and skill because of the higher risk and lack of control that having single pieces so vulnerable entails. We confront here a familiar theme, as the literal and figurative exposure of such single pieces to the possibility of domination by an opponent's single piece is equated explicitly with risk. Conversely, in this form as well as in *portes*, when a player is in the advantageous position of having two pieces situated safely before an open expanse of stations the opponent must begin to traverse, the player often points to these pieces and says with a satisfied smile to spectators, "They're policing" ("*kanune astinomia*"), which carries a corresponding air of watchfulness, on the lookout for any exposed piece by the opponent.

The final form, *portes* ("doors"; the games usually are played continuously in the following order: *portes, plakoto, fevga*), is the same as that most often played in the United States, where single pieces are not frozen but captured and sent back to the farthest point (eighteen stations away) from the end quarter of the board. Most of my contacts saw *portes* negatively in comparison to the other forms, both because it is in their eyes the form of *tavli* most influenced by luck and also because it is identified with tourists as many of them encounter the ubiquitous *tavli* boards at the old harbor's cafés and play, to the Chaniots, only the "simplistic" *portes*. Despite, or perhaps because of, the high degree of luck the game is seen as entailing, many of my fellow *tavli* players also saw *portes* as a somewhat predictable game after the first few moves by both players. The key here is that for good players the strategy of *portes* is almost standardized, such that the opening dice rolls can quickly give either player a clear advantage. The tourists' predictable familiarity with this "simple" form rather than others makes them doubly passive in Chaniots' eyes: Not only do they play a game where the luck decides more than skill who has the advantage, but the game also provides yet another example of how all tourists are alike (matching their perceived homogeneity of preferences in such things as food, accommodations, and entertainment).

The expansive gestures and loud exclamations, combined with the distinctive noise of the *tavli* dice and pieces, mark the playing of the game and the players' attitude toward it as very different from that of poker, discussed in chapter 3. There, the consequences of the exposure of one's intentions are heightened by the profit to be made from reading another's situation well in the context of a limited amount of (visible) information. In *tavli*, by contrast, everything relevant in the game is visible and at least potentially appreciable; all the pieces are in view, and the dice are rolled and watched carefully by spectators and players. The key in *tavli* is not just to see what is on the board but to see what is *happening* on the board, not only what pieces are vulnerable but such things as what obvious options might lead one to overlook others, as the apparent openness is misleading. Nikos, my mentor in *tavli*, when I had missed an obvious (to him) opportunity to make a devastating move, exclaimed with frustration, "You're not seeing!" (*"Dhen vlepis!"*), and the phrase could not more clearly illustrate that although in *tavli* one makes one's moves with sound and fury, one must watch one's opponent's moves and the board's subtleties, and the audible must not detract one from the visible. To exploit this concatenation of the senses, *tavli* players use styles of play that combine both of these components, creating a busy atmosphere that overlays the still board and its pieces.

Among the youth of Chania, backgammon is an arena for the playing out of gender relations, and the game's foregrounding of expressions of dominance and inequality provides ample opportunities for more and less explicit expressions of power between them. One occasion that demonstrated this element of the game to me, which was not unusual, was an overheard exchange between two women who were playing backgammon together and a young man they evidently knew who was sitting at the next table. The man commented critically on almost every move one of the young women made and ignored her repeated efforts to get him to be quiet. The parallel is obvious: Even though he was not playing, the man used precisely the same tactic of a verbal barrage that is the core of the attempts to misdirect opponents from the board itself during the game. A similar link might be found between this tactic and ones deployed in the domestic sphere in Greece, where I often overheard or witnessed similar usage of verbal exclamations, often but not exclusively by men, to drown out and exclude opposing views by members of the opposite sex.

In another case, I observed how a triangle between three young people of Chania played itself out over a *tavli* board. The two men and one woman were all friends of each other and of me, and I spent many an afternoon playing *tavli* or watching games between them. We all played each other, but between Yiannis and Kostas the games were a continuing saga. We played at the café where Yiannis worked, a place in the old town but slightly distant from the continuously busy old harbor; here the afternoons were mostly quiet and there were rarely other customers there to observe the games. Always the previous encounter's ending score could be recalled, and talk about it often led to another round. When I arrived early one such afternoon Yiannis could not wait to demonstrate to me the ending of a game I had not seen the previous day; he set the pieces up on the board and demonstrated how, in the decisive game (they had been tied four games apiece), he had been in a terrible position and the game looked beyond his reach, when he rolled double fours (*dortia*) three times in succession to win the game dramatically. Because Yiannis often had complained that Kostas had often been the recipient of more than his share of good luck in their previous games, Yiannis said it was fitting that he finally won an important game with "good dice."

After some time, Maria and Kostas began dating, and they spent more and more time together, but our regular afternoon get-togethers did not change. Soon a triangle emerged, however, as I began to see Maria and Yiannis together on occasion, although never in the central part of Chania and always while Kostas was working. My conversations with Maria and Yiannis confirmed that, although Maria still intended to keep dating Kostas, she and Yiannis had, as it were, enjoyed each other's company, and whereas Yiannis was interested in continuing the affair, she was ambivalent about this possibility and was concerned that Kostas not find out that anything had happened. All this intrigue gave Kostas's and Yiannis's battles over the *tavli* board extra levels of meaning, as Yiannis never hesitated to make a pun that became extra sharp given his affair with Maria. For example, Yiannis's references to taking Kostas's pieces (*poulia*) in particular heightened the tension in the air because of the danger of one stray comment exposing all. But there was a further level of uncertainty because it was not out of the realm of possibility that Kostas knew about the affair and simply chose to read the comments at the level of the game only. The tension of doubt pervaded the games. What did Kostas know about what was going on? Weeks later, it seemed he knew nothing: He and Maria had broken up (for other reasons) yet remained good friends. Maria and Yiannis did not continue their affair, and we all began to see each other less.

Luck and Skill in Tavli

In the context of this social indeterminacy *tavli*'s interplay of luck and skill provides one arena where personal claims to the ability to engage uncertainty are made. In this domain, the term *tikhi* is most often used to denote "luck," and this word most closely approximates the English "luck" (in contrast to other forms, such as *gouri,* explored in chapter 3). Skill here is *tekhni,* and again the translation of this word is fairly direct, and this contrast mirrors that made between "skill" and "luck" as categories of games, a distinction both Chaniots and many in the United States make. The generally positive evaluation of any demonstration of skill and the negative evaluation of reliance on luck are a constant but not immutable presence over the table. Thus, a player who, rolling the dice, seeks to escape dire circumstances by coming through with the only result that would turn the game around will be told, "You're so lucky" (*"Ise toso tikheros!"*) or called "Wide-ass!" (*"Kolofardhe!"*).[7] A noticeably recurring streak of luck can be turned to the player's advantage, however, as in the case of Stavros. Stavros proudly adopted the appellation *kolofardhos* and applied it to all areas of his life, such as in his motorcycle riding: "Yes, I drive fast, but I won't have an accident, because I'm a *kolofardhos.*" After he had an accident, Stavros's conviction was unshaken, and his inherent luckiness now accounted for his surviving with minor injuries.

But this distinction between skill and luck is not always so clear, and it is through a clever association with good dice rolls that a player can make the luckiest result seem tied to his or her own prowess. A player may predict what will happen on the next roll, either specifically, "Come on, double fives!" (*"Ela, pendares!"*), or generally, "Now you'll see some fun!" (*"Tora tha dhis plaka!"*), saying this just before tossing the dice across the board. If a good roll occurs, or, more rarely, the exact roll predicted occurs, then the distinction between luck and skill becomes, at least for the moment, difficult to maintain. This performative feat is not one of simple cause and effect, as the actual influence of the player's call over the outcome is always fundamentally unclear. Rather, the close association of prediction and result connects the player's ability to engage chance with the luck that may govern the roll of the dice. The key here is that, as in poker (where one's claim about the overall patterns of winning and losing constitutes a claim about one's own privileged position vis-à-vis chance; see chapter 3), so here this claim to be able to "call" what will happen on the next roll is a risk that can pay off by tying the player to the indeterminacy of the game itself.

This, finally, is the dominant trope of accountability of the backgammon board, the interplay between claims to having luck and claims to having skill. With the contest and the game board itself in view of everyone, with one's skill not just at the game but also at its embodied gestures and vocalization on constant display, and finally with the regular outcomes of the dice rolls also subject to scrutiny, it is both fitting and ironic that the performative goal seems to be to make the role of the chancy dice and one's own skill nearly indistinguishable by this rhetorical legerdemain. Again, what is at stake is the position of the gambler with respect to the influences on the game, skill and luck, the ideal being to present oneself convincingly as perfectly situated at the nexus of both.

In a conversation with Nikos, we began to talk about playing *tavli* and the point of view of the two players. It was then that Nikos made the same analogy I had heard once before. To play *tavli*, or any game, he said, is like the *proxenio*, the first meeting between the bride and groom and their families in arranged Cretan weddings. The first time at the wife's house, he said, everyone watches how the groom eats, whether he eats quickly or slowly, with his hands or not, and all watch how the bride serves everything. This searching out of the behavior of the other is at the heart of playing a game between two people in public view, especially with *tavli*, he said.

This idea is linked to another I encountered in Chania. During another conversation with Nikos (the full context of which is provided in chapter 6), he paused and looked at me gravely and said, "The biggest risk in life is friendship" (*"To pio meghalo risko sti zoi ine i filia"*), and in ensuing conversations other Chaniots echoed this sentiment. Much as in the *proxenio*, where before opening their family to admit a new member people attempt to read from the actions and words of relative strangers something about their qualities, so in friendship, he told me, one must learn from reading from the other's actions whether to trust that person by allowing him or her entry into one's life. "Someone can always do you wrong," the gambler said, "and how can you know the other? To begin a friendship is to risk everything."[8]

Notes

1. *Thanasis* is a game similar to rummy but with many wild cards and two decks. See the Appendix for a more complete description of the rules and conventions of these games.

2. In this way the theme of eating is identified closely with stealing, an issue addressed by Herzfeld in the context of animal theft (1985, 22 and passim).

3. This pattern runs in direct contrast to historical information about backgammon as played under Islamic rule, as Crete was for a large part of its history. Franz Rosenthal notes that backgammon (*nard* in Arabic) is associated in Islamic historical documentation quite closely with the Arabic root *q-m-r*, meaning gambling. *Koumari* is derived from this same root, through its Turkish form, and there seems to be a similar use of the root to refer both to gambling generally and to dicing specifically. In any case, *nard* or *tavli* is second only to chess in its frequency of appearance with references to *q-m-r* in the Islamic texts (Rosenthal 1975, 34–35, 40–42).

4. As I have for all of the gamblers mentioned in this work, I use pseudonyms for places of business where gambling takes place.

5. The use of the continuous form of this verb here (perhaps more clearly if clumsily translated as "Keep playing!") highlights the ongoing and as yet undetermined outcome of the unfolding game.

6. The word *poulí* in Greek is also slang for "penis," but I found that in the context of *tavli* it was used in the way described earlier.

7. A consistent account of why this term in Chania denotes luckiness over the gaming table was not forthcoming from Chaniots, but there was a pattern in the responses that suggested that a "wide-ass" is one who spends all available time just sitting and playing, thus gaining the benefit of lucky streaks through a sacrifice of success in other domains of life. Although I am aware of the term's broader usage elsewhere in Greece, I cannot account for this apparent narrowness of usage in Chania.

8. Although Herzfeld has noted the perception of relations between kin as more fraught with a certain kind of risk than friendship (1991, 163), his point is subtly different from mine. Herzfeld discusses how kinsfolk are perceived as more likely to take advantage of each other than friends, something I also encountered in Chania, whereas here I am concerned with the risk involved in opening up one's potentially damaging secrets to another, a shift in the level of intimacy between people who are not related, a situation in which choice becomes a key issue, whereas one cannot as easily chose one's relatives. These examples provide a clear sense of the terms behind social interaction in Chania, the social stakes that permeate everyday experience.

3   *Poker and Positioning*

Early in my research in Chania, I watched a poker game at Meltemi, the gambling coffeehouse introduced at the start of this book, while Petros was its owner. Playing that evening were Petros and several other regulars: Nondas (the later owner of the establishment), Mikhalis, and Stelios. The game lasted for almost five hours, and throughout the game Nondas had been losing and Stelios had been winning, and doing so soundly. There seemed to be no end to his production of flushes, straights, and even a few fours-of-a-kind. Stelios seemed not to react at all to his good fortune; he played steadily and before long had a sizable pile of markers in front of him. After this continued for some time, Nondas turned to no one in particular and shouted, "He's made monkeys of us!" Then, as he cut for the next deal, he said to the deck of cards forcefully, "Wake up, bastard!"

Such an event was one among many such forceful attempts to engage fortune that I observed in Chania. How is the social analyst to make sense of them? Does the appearance of such "superstitious" practices indicate an ignorance or stubborn intransigence about integrating laws of probability into Chaniot gamblers' understandings of outcomes? Or do such events provide an opportunity for social analysts to understand more clearly how in the present, as outcomes appear from moment to moment, social actors engage them and construct understandings of their world, understandings that are bound up in relationships of power and interest? In this chapter I explore the microsocial interaction that takes place over a poker table as a way of clarifying the extent to which the interpretations of outcomes by those players reflects an ongoing project of the construction of a meaningful world. Anthony Giddens's theory of structuration provides a backdrop for reconsidering the place of contingency in social life not simply in "modern" settings but in any environment where the unexpected unfolds. The broader argument is that practices and concepts often treated by anthropologists as respected but exotic modes of thought or action, isolated from questions of power and "modern" practice in general, can be instead the sites and keystones of the ongoing projects of reality construction themselves. As Michael Jackson (1989, 17) writes about the reliance by anthropologists on such categories as witchcraft, the evil eye, and magic, "Many of these frames of reference suggest radical *discontinuities* between 'them' and 'us,' and fail to clarify on what grounds we can reach an understanding of such 'alien' beliefs and practices." It is for this reason that discussions of risk analysis and management on one hand and superstitious practices on the other often present themselves as incommensurable.

Risk, Modernity, and Structuration

The kind of dichotomy I identify here between nonmodern (or premodern) views of uncertainty and the modern view—that which takes the analytical status of risk as preeminent—are evident in Anthony Giddens's *Modernity and Self-Identity: Self and Society in the Late Modern Age* (1991). The work is a useful example because it demonstrates clearly the dangers of residual categories that appear inevitably once the West is identified with an inherent quality. Modernity for Giddens is defined by three necessary preconditions: industrialization, capitalism, and surveillance and control of social life (epitomized by the nation-state). He concludes that members of modern societies are characterized by an awareness of the uncertainty of future outcomes, which are in turn shaped by the prevalence of such statistical techniques as risk assessment. Conversely, in "nonmodern" societies, Giddens argues, there is a concern with fate, destiny, and an individual's relation to the cosmos (*fortuna*). Thus, Giddens equates "traditional" society with a preoccupation with the cosmological domain while denying its members the possibility of doubting their cosmology. Thinking in terms of risk assessment (which Giddens opposes to thinking in terms of *fortuna*) therefore is unavailable in these societies, Giddens suggests, because it is "intrinsic to institutionalized risk systems" which are "much more prominent in modern rather than premodern societies" (1991, 119, 117). The conditions of modern societies, on the other hand, require that their members think in terms of risk assessment, although notions of fate "do not disappear altogether" (130).[1]

In essentializing such categories as risk, fate, *fortuna*, fatalism, and modernity, Giddens relies on a highly individualized focus throughout his discussion. Giddens separates the individual from his or her social context, just as he separates the concept of modernity from its historical context. This forces Giddens to essentialize both these concepts and the people who seem to act completely at their mercy. Consider the following quote: "The point, to repeat, is not that day-to-day life is inherently more risky than was the case in previous eras. It is rather that, in conditions of modernity, for lay actors as well as for experts in specific fields, thinking in terms of risk assessment is a more or less ever-present exercise, of a partly imponderable character. . . . Individuals seek to colonize a future for themselves as an intrinsic part of their life-planning. . . . All individuals establish a portfolio of risk assessment" (1991, 123–24, 125). This is precisely the assumption that leads Giddens to equate the lack of a highly rationalized, bureaucratized system of risk assessment (as found in his premodern societies) to an adherence to an outlook based on fate, or predestination (Giddens 1991, 109–43). This perspective denies the possibility that fate could be appealed to as a strategy, one made possible by circumstance according to the rules of performative appropriateness. Thus, Giddens's formulation does not hold for a place such as Chania, where a discourse of fate is not prevalent among most gamblers but instead appears in the Greek state's ad campaigns for its several lotteries, most pointedly in the poster that proclaimed, "It puts your fate in your hands!" Gamblers in Chania, by contrast, found an appeal to fate less attractive precisely because it suggested a lack of agency ("Fate means you close your eyes!" one exclaimed to me).

One reviewer of his earlier work suggests that Giddens's key contribution to anthropological thought is his integration of action and structure (Karp 1986). Ironically, it is precisely on this point that I find Giddens's later work on risk and fate less successful. The reason for this is that Giddens relies on ideas of fate and risk that lack any sense of potential manipulation by the actors themselves (in direct contrast to his earlier model of structuration, which accorded social actors this ability). The pervasiveness and inevitability of risk assessment thinking in modernity and notions of fate elsewhere that Giddens observes may be more the result of his own exposure to the prevalence of such ideas in the social sciences. This general observation is also made by Jackson (1989, 15), who, as I mentioned in the Introduction, proposes that uncertainty is a universal feature of human experience, arguing that "the anthropologist's preoccupation with regularity, pattern, system, and structure has to be seen as less an objective reflection of social reality than a comment on his personal and professional need for certitude and order."[2] I therefore view *modernity* as a problematic term when used analytically to distinguish some societies from others—Greece might well be placed on either side, depending on how the line is drawn—and make the argument here and throughout this book for an alternative approach to making sense of the place of the contingent in any society.

Not surprisingly, then, turning to Giddens's earlier work provides a more helpful approach, and it is with regard to this work that Karp's observations above are well-founded. In *The Constitution of Society* (1984), Giddens outlines his theory of structuration, an approach that relies on the notion that local actors are themselves discursively and practically knowledgeable about their activities (they are as much, here, social theorists as the social scientists who study them). Giddens's restatement of his theory bears extensive quotation:

> Structure, as recursively organized sets of rules and resources, is out of time and space, save in its instantiations and co-ordination as memory traces, and is marked by an "absence of the subject." The social systems in which structure is recursively implicated, on the contrary, comprise the situated activities of human agents, reproduced across time and space. Analysing the structuration of social systems means studying the modes in which such systems, grounded in the knowledgeable activities of situated actors who draw upon rules and resources in the diversity of action contexts, are produced and reproduced in interaction. . . . The constitution of agents and structures are not two independently given sets of phenomena, a dualism, but represent a duality. . . . [T]he structural properties of social systems are both medium and outcome of the practices they recursively organize. (1984, 25)

As they engage in activities, then, human beings "draw upon rules and resources in the diversity of action contexts" and thereby produce and reproduce the social systems of which they are a part. Therefore, *structuration* indicates a dynamic relationship between structure and action, where amid the semistructured flow of everyday life, knowledgeable actors' practices both shape and reproduce those structures. It is in this sense that the concept of structuration can be applied to a social setting where uncertainty is a key (and explicit) element. Thus, we may usefully explore the means by which gamblers make sense of unforeseen outcomes as they unfold in the context of a game, while concomitantly relating these understandings to other aspects of social life, by applying this idea of structuration. Moreover, such an approach can be extended to apply to any case where the politics of contingency are at stake. Giddens (1984, 25–26) himself observes this: "Structure is not to be equated with constraint but is always both constraining and enabling. This, of course, does not . . . compromise the possibility that actors' own theories of the social systems which they help to constitute and reconstitute in their activities may reify those systems. The reification of social relations, or the discursive 'naturalization' of the historically contingent circumstances and products of human action, is one of the main dimensions of ideology in social life." Therefore, a recognition of actors' awareness of the possibility of "unintended consequences" becomes crucial (1984, 27) because it is this sensitivity to the contingent that makes the process of creating meaning a high-stakes enterprise.[3] Structuration allows the analyst to grasp what is at stake in various actors' putting forth of particular means for understanding the unexpected. With this in mind, then, I now turn to an examination of this phenomenon in practice.

Life Is a Gamble

In Chania, a frequent subject for chatter between games at the poker tables in the coffeehouses, or *kafenia*, was a certain type of "luck" (*gouri*) or, more specifically, various players' claims to possessing or lacking it and their attributions of this presence or lack in others. These claims and attributions, and attempts to maintain or alter their verity, reveal as much about the immediate social milieu as they do about the player in question. The concept of *gouri* often is encountered in discussions with gamblers outside the immediate context of playing, although it is often behind the scenes at the gaming table during the game, as will become clear later in this chapter.

One might be tempted to translate *gouri* as "lucky charm," but it is far more general: Anything from a time of day to a particular position at the card table to a semiritualized practice (always drinking a Greek coffee before playing, for example) to the presence (or absence) of someone can bring a player good or bad *gouri*. The entire immediate social scene (for example, that of a coffeehouse) can be claimed to bring one *gouri*. For Chaniots, *gouri* has a connotation similar to the English word *augur*, where the idea of a "sign" or "omen" of good tidings is not far removed from how *gouri* is used and often suggests an indication of this good fortune in a proximate item, person, or practice.[4] On several occasions, after I arrived at a *kafenio* and sat slightly behind a friend who was playing poker, that player began winning. He then referred to it often, saying, "Bravo! Look! You brought me *gouri*!" The impetus behind and meaning of this claim was later brought into focus by how one player described it to me: "Someone who is winning doesn't want to change anything, because he doesn't want to change his *gouri.*" There is a direct parallel here with Giddens's observation that in many instances of social life "strategically placed actors seek reflectively to regulate the overall conditions of system reproduction either to keep things as they are or to change them" (1984, 27–28); the importance of this aspect of the application of *gouri* will become evident through the example discussed later in this chapter.

Poker is an especially useful focus for an examination of how *gouri* is used because the structural features of this game (i.e., that it is a contest between a small number of people who play together over an extended period of time and that its central strategic element is one of hiding and revealing, both of cards and intentions) help bring into sharp relief this intersection between *gouri* and social interaction. It is in the context of an unpredictably unfolding present and an indeterminate future that players (dis)order the reality over the gaming table through their claims about how the emerging patterns of outcomes, and their position with regard to them, should be understood. These claims themselves constitute risks of the self as they expose the player who makes them to the possibility of damaging social remonstration. Also, I want to be sure to note that I emphasize here one trope of accountability, in this case *gouri,* somewhat to the exclusion of others (skill, luck as otherwise construed, fate, and statistical probability). Although these other tropes emerge in poker-playing contexts and play a part in my discussion in this chapter, I nonetheless found that in the context of poker *gouri* is most frequently highlighted. Therefore, I here extend Chaniots' emphasis on *gouri* for the heuristic purpose of further illustrating the degree to which claims about chance through this term are embedded in local social relations.

An Evening of Contest

The event described here took place in late November at Meltemi, a poker *kafenio*[5] that I visited regularly. In the evenings, beginning around 7 P.M., the poker started, often lasting until midnight or 1 A.M. On most nights there was one table with a continuous game, almost always the front left table, as a heavy curtain covered the window along the front of the *kafenio,* leaving this table the least visible from the road. This position highlighted the tension between exposure and concealment, the public and the private, that is as present at the boundaries between the gambling *kafenio* and the outside world as it is over the poker table itself. In the months before I made a contact at this *kafenio* I had walked by it many times, catching only the barest glimpse through the windowed doorway of a card game at that front table before I was already past it and wondering whether I had been seen staring. There were four players who played for about eight hours on this particular evening. Petros, a close contact of mine and the former owner of Meltemi (having sold it the previous spring, 1995, to Nondas), was there. Petros had nonetheless continued to play at Meltemi nearly every night. Because either Nondas or Petros played in nearly every game (and sometimes both together), one of the two was the "banker," an arrangement that did not change after the sale of the *kafenio*. Another player at the table this evening, to the right of Petros, was Mikhalis, another regular. He was a quiet player, and seemingly very serious, as he never seemed to change expression, whether winning or losing, and even between hands he did not engage in the frequently heard chatter over the table.

The third player at the table (to Mikhalis's right) was Andreas, a young man whom I had not seen before at the *kafenio*. He was about thirty-two years old, and therefore about fifteen years younger than the approximate age of the other players. Petros later called him a *khroniaris*, which means someone who plays "yearly," that is, during the holiday season. However, the word is also used for young livestock, in much the same way that *yearling* is used in English, and this evocation of qualities of vulnerability, naiveté, and youth highlights how regular gamblers often characterize their relationship with the *khroniaridhes* as predatory. This portrayal cuts both ways, however, because a yearling who is fortunate enough (in the regulars' eyes) to win over the short holiday period of gambling, and who then disappears, does not give the regulars a chance to win their money back. Though not a novice at the game, Andreas did seem at times to suffer from lapses in concentration, making procedural mistakes such as trying to change the ante when he was dealer before a full round had passed or forgetting who had opened and therefore having to ask the other players who could bet first in the second round. Nonetheless, Andreas won steadily over the course of the evening, presenting a seemingly endless string of threes-of-a-kind. The link between these outcomes and the broader issues of intergenerational contest and contest between novices and regulars figured prominently through the implicitly and explicitly applied trope of *gouri* as the evening went on. The fourth player, Dhimitris, was not as regular a patron as Petros and Mikhalis, but I had seen him at the *kafenio* a few times, and he had been playing there for a little over a year, albeit semiregularly (a few times a month, he told me). He was roughly the same age as Petros and Mikhalis, and again the difference not simply in familiarity between the players but also in age, between Andreas and the other three, was clear.

As play proceeded through the evening, Petros was breaking even or losing slightly, Mikhalis was a little in the black, Andreas was winning almost without pause, and Dhimitris seemed to lose hand after hand, most often to Andreas. Mikhalis, as always, kept his expression the same, nearly silent as he asked for cards, bet, or folded. Andreas's miscues continued, and responses by all of the players to them grew more abrupt and impatient, but it was Dhimitris who began to take every opportunity to complain. After losing a high-stakes hand that had come down to only him and Andreas (Andreas's full house beating Dhimitris' three-of-a-kind), he turned to Petros and quickly showed him his cards before throwing them in, and said, "Look! What else could I have done? He doesn't know what's going on but he wins!" Getting a very small nod from Petros, Dhimitris continued, "That wasn't correct, what I did? I had three queens!" Andreas remained silent, not even looking at Dhimitris, who continued to look around the *kafenio,* his arms slightly spread, a mixture of bewilderment, anger, and supplication on his face. At that point Mikhalis, who was shuffling and preparing to deal the next round, looked up for a moment and said sharply, "Come now! Are we playing or talking?" This ended the discussion, and the next hand was played. The pattern of winning and losing, the disruption of Dhimitris's outburst, and the difference in age and familiarity between the players combined here to create a situation that on the surface may be simple but that in fact reveals what is at stake during this game beyond the money on the table. Before returning to analyze this event more closely, however, I will take some space to note some significant and unusual features of the game as it is played in Chania. Given the importance the trope of *gouri* places on circumstance and practice, these conventional aspects of the game are central to a full understanding of what happened that evening and how it provides an example of structuration in practice.

How Can One Know Another?

The poker game they played that night in Meltemi was by far the most common form of it played there and throughout Chania, and in almost all respects it is the same as draw poker as commonly played in the United States.[6] Between hands, the deal rotates around the table counterclockwise. After one complete cycle has been completed the dealer has the right to change the minimum opening bid or increase the ante. However, the ante is handled differently than in most draw poker games as played in the United States. In Chania it is the dealer who puts in a certain amount, not each player, and this amount is forfeited to the next hand if the hand dealt is tossed in (that is, not opened by anyone). A certain amount of money is paid to the house, and this is called the *vidhani*.

In Meltemi *kafenio* they also have an unusual system for representing the money bet on the table. Rather than the more commonly used poker chips, this *kafenio* uses *khartakia* ("little cards"). The owner takes the old decks that have become unusable because of the marks from wear on their backs and takes them to a friend who, with a machine, trims off the white border around each card.[7] The trimmed-down cards, each representing 250 Dr (about US$1), are to the players noticeably smaller than the full-sized ones and do not create confusion for them. To the unwitting, however, it can seem that the players are playing a rather strange game where they periodically throw cards into the middle of the table. The beauty of the system, the owner told me, is that "when the police come, they will see that we are just playing cards!" Here, then, the theme of concealment and revelation is played out not between the players at the table but rather between them and those outside this social sphere, most notably the police, who do not participate in the game.[8] This tension between gambling as hidden practice and the attempts by the state to regulate it (through both its enforcement of antigambling laws and its sponsorship of casinos and state lottery games) reappears throughout the concealed scenes of illegal gambling in Chania and brings to mind the difference, noted earlier, between local gamblers' conceptions of the risks they take and the state's use of the trope of fate in its advertising for these games.

There is also an instructive difference between the characterization of the group of players at the poker table as a closed community with regard to others in the *kafenio* and the sharply different ethos of the table in many other Greek contexts, where, as Cowan (1990, 148) notes, "a mere lack of chairs cannot justify exclusion. Normally, as the proverb says, 'At the table, there's room for all but one—Satan himself!' " In poker, by contrast, there is a high degree of sensitivity to outside influence on the part of many players, who often insist that no spectators sit near or behind them. Even players who tolerate spectators insist that they sit back from the table, out of the direct illumination of the lamp suspended above. One such player turned quickly to me during a game and looked down, saying sharply, "Don't do that!" It took me a moment to realize that he was speaking of my foot, which was propped on a crossrung of his chair. My delay in understanding was the result of the fact that this practice is so common in *kafenia* and often is an expression of commensal intimacy (particularly in the midst of a good conversation), coupled with the fact that this was someone I knew fairly well. I immediately realized that this was a very different situation, one in which normal conventions are subordinated to those of the game.[9]

This bounded quality of the table mirrors the bounded nature of the game itself, where all of the players share the intent of creating the appropriate conditions for the unpredictable outcomes to unfold. The game thus takes on a sacrosanct quality, where a significant breach of protocol (such as an extra card dealt) means the hand is "broken" (*spasmeno*) and must be thrown out, with all money returned to the appropriate players. The role of the dealer becomes especially important here because his recommendations for the rectification of more minor transgressions (such as misunderstandings about the amount a given player has tossed in) are the ones likely to be followed. Albeit temporarily, the dealer is the authority at the table, and it is his job to ensure that the game unfolds without contamination by error or cheating.

The four players also regularly (re)determine who will sit where. Four differently ranked cards are selected from the deck and mixed up, face down, on the table. Each player draws a card and they turn them over; they then arrange themselves around the table from lowest rank to highest. The positions are shuffled in this way every two hours so that no one player enjoys a regular advantage by, for example, always following a player with whose style he is very familiar. One player serves as the banker, selling stacks of twenty khartakia for 5,000 Dr (about US$20) each. This player, usually the owner or a good friend of his, and also having carefully placed stacks of twenty khartakia on a nearby small table, does not move for these reshufflings of position, so the other players organize themselves around him. Now and then this leads to disagreements because one player or another may be particularly happy with his spot, most often because he has been winning and he claims it has brought him *gouri*. In the end, though, the changes are made, and play continues. In one such case, Khronis, another taxi driver who often played at Meltemi, hit upon an ingenious compromise when Petros refused his request not to shift places: He picked up his chair and moved it to the new spot, insisting that "it was the chair, surely." The rest of their time playing Khronis kept that chair whenever places shifted and his claim was borne out; his winning streak continued the entire evening.

Many kinds of things are alternately hidden and revealed in the game of poker, and understanding this quality is essential for an examination of the game as a forum for the engagement of chance. The emphasis placed on reading the other players while giving away nothing (or false information) gives the game a special status with some of its players. One of them, an older and well-known *koumartzis* (gambler, though with a slightly dramatic quality) in Chania, in running through a list of card games and classifying them to me as "skill" or "luck" games, hesitated before classifying poker: "It's not a luck or skill game; it is . . . let's say . . . psychological," he said. In general the regular players of poker to whom I spoke noted that the game demanded something extra and that this made the game, in their eyes, different from and better than other kinds of gambling. That this characterization of poker by its players is as much an attempt to claim some special access to this skill as it is to distinguish the game from others does not render these claims trivial. On the contrary, devoted players of each of the major forms of gambling in Chania commonly took steps to distinguish their game (and therefore themselves) from the others around, a practice that mirrors the distinctions made by those who play only in private gambling clubs regarding coffeehouse gambling and vice versa (see chapter 2).

The distinctive skill in poker is the ability to read the other players' intentions, gauge their resources, both in money and self-confidence, notice patterns in their actions, and, finally, have a good idea of the quality of the cards they are holding, independent of the deceptively large (or small) amount of money on the table. All of this must be done with corresponding control over what oneself reveals in the overriding context of unpredictable distributions of cards. Although most gamblers seem to be trying to give away nothing—indeed, a poker game seems at first to be almost devoid of any communication apart from the betting—it would be a grave mistake to take this at face value. As all the players attempt to limit their behavior, they each attempt to read patterns of action in other players, such as changes in a player's tempo of play or betting gesture; the importance of the most minute action is magnified. All of the action at the table is very constrained, but it nonetheless fills a range of expression, from enthusiasm to boredom, sharpness to weariness, confidence to worry—any one of which may be falsely adopted or accurately attributed. Thus the game behind the game in poker is one of strategic concealment and disclosure as one attempts to give others an inscrutable posture while simultaneously making one's own guesses about other players' situations.

Particularly relevant in poker, and an attempt to conceal just this kind of dangerous self-revelation, is the attempt to adopt the stance of "the player" (*o pekhtis*).[10] This image, remarkably consistent in its portrayal to me by various contacts, encompasses the tuxedo-clad, James Bond–like master of the game,[11] with a serious, distant, unconcernedness or lack of emotionality. A clear instance of the first part of this image was driven home to me on my first day in Athens when, in the midst of

Syntagma Square, the political center of Athens, I looked up at the scaffolding surrounding a large hotel only to see an advertisement for a Greek
male singer's latest album, *O Pekhtis*. The advertisement was a three-
story-high picture of the album cover printed onto the scaffolding's wind
cover, and it showed a lavish casino with the tuxedo-clad singer at a
roulette table in the foreground, with a revealingly dressed woman back-
lit at a doorway in the background. The *pekhtis* is someone who does not
concern himself with the possible outcomes in a gambling situation,
good or bad. This ideal of unconcernedness, of what I call instrumental
nonchalance, is paradoxically effectual because it is the lack of concern
over winning that brings success. This idea is consistent with what Herzfeld (1991, 168–76) calls the "ethos of imprecision," where those engaged
in social relations evince a casualness about monetary exactitude, an
"economic carelessness," such as in financial or other exchange transactions between neighbors, kin, or friends. The difference here is that a
transaction between individuals is not necessary for one to have an opportunity to present this posture. Instead, any risky situation provides
one a chance to appear unconcerned and paradoxically more likely to
attain one's objective. In the example given earlier, Mikhalis was a player
who fit this image, but his inconsistency in winning and losing led several of my informants to avoid classifying him as a *pekhtis*. "He plays
well," one said, "but he's too careful." The line a true "player" must walk
between daring and care is fine indeed.

The game is further informed by individuals' past experiences of playing together; several of them had done so for many years. Thus Petros was
able quickly to characterize the competence of several of the regulars at
the *kafenio*. In discussing Yiannis, a friendly and expansive regular at
Meltemi (although he as often sat and watched or read as played), Petros
said that "he does not know the game well. He doesn't know how to control how fast or slow he plays, and he reveals the quality of his hand by
pausing or not pausing." By contrast, Nikos, another regular, was to Petros a good player but too conservative. Finally, he said that Nondas, once
he was owner of Meltemi, tried too hard to continue to make money playing, often losing his entire night's *vidhani* in a couple of hours. An important caveat to this applies, however. In Chania, particular gambling
kafenia are associated with two primary features: type of game and identity of players. Thus, Meltemi *kafenio* had a modest reputation for mid-
level stakes poker, not known to all the gamblers with whom I spoke but
known to the majority. Its customers were primarily working-class Chaniots, many of them tourist industry workers and taxi drivers. (The *kafenio*'s proximity to the largest taxi stand in Chania accounts for the sec-

ond category.) But in contrast to many characterizations of (nongambling) coffeehouses in the Greek ethnographic literature (such as that of Papataxiarchis [1991]), the makeup of the gambling *kafenia* in Chania was changeable from evening to evening. I was struck by the frequency with which I was asked by certain gamblers for the name of someone else in the *kafenio*, someone I assumed they knew fairly well.

This transience has a double meaning among the gambling community, as I discussed briefly in chapter 1. On one hand, a gambler may brag about the number of *kafenia* in which he is welcome, as my friend Charis did during a long afternoon and evening in which we stopped at five different *kafenia* in Chania. At two of them he knew the owner or other regulars through his ties to the political party *Sinaspismos*; two others were popular with people from the area around his village, Skines; and the last *kafenio* was near where he had owned a furniture store. At the same time, this familiarity with multiple sites may justify a negative characterization of him as someone who chooses where to play on a given night solely on the basis of where there might be a profitable combination of money and skill. The degree to which poker players may be able to read others because of past history is somewhat limited by this variability of patronage. Of course, this shifting of opponents becomes fertile ground for claims to being able all the more quickly to evaluate one's adversaries.

There is also a noticeable distinction between the play of the hand and the periods between hands, which provide regular breaks from the near silence and constitute a comparative flourish of communication. It is here that one most immediately encounters claims about *gouri*. The practice of concealment and disclosure can take on more explicit forms at this time, too, as players who folded show what terrible hands they had (or how they should have stayed in), others pull a few more cards from the deck until they see what they would have received had they decided to throw away cards rather than hold what they had, and the winner gathers in his *khartakia*, stacking them or piling them in front of him. Petros often threw the card from his hand that would have completed an otherwise worthless straight or full house toward the hand of the player who had just thrown it down in disgust.

All Is Right with the World

To return to the concept of *gouri*, then, and to the vignette presented earlier, who speaks and who does not during the breaks between hands is influenced by the trends of winning and losing over the course of play that evening. During these breaks the contest over claims about the reasons for the outcomes breaks out explicitly, and it is here that the idea of *gouri* comes most prominently into play, as it did for Andreas and Dhimitris. The risk of self that making these claims entails constitutes a self-exposure, the staking of a claim about not simply the players around the table but also about how the shifting patterns of outcomes themselves should be understood and how they should be understood in the context of broader social relations, such as between the "yearlings" and the regulars. What is at stake, then, for the players is not simply the money on the table. It is the momentary, ephemeral, but no less potent ordering of reality. As in this example, it is the player who has just lost a fair amount (and possibly also been losing steadily up to that point) who is most likely to risk breaking the silence and perform his loss. Things clearly were not going well for Dhimitris, who had been losing steadily. To change his *gouri*, he needed to shake things up in some way. Monetary loss thus becomes an index for a particular, and damaging, status vis-à-vis chance rather than simply revealing a loss of financial capital.

Although hands end in different ways, most often the two rounds of bidding leave two players betting against each other, with the other two having folded along the way. Thus, after each hand the most common situation is one in which one of the four players has just lost more than the others, and one has won. The player who won would invite direct reprisals, and potential conflict, by boasting, as Andreas would have from Dhimitris in this case. Speaking would thus violate the winner's interest in keeping things as they are; if something about the situation and his actions in it has brought him some *gouri*, then he does not want to change a thing. In this respect, the *fact* of winning is an indication that the immediate social situation (and, by implication, the player's position within it and interpretation of it) is felicitous (in the Austinian sense; see Austin 1975 [1956]); that is, "all is right with the world," including the winner's view of and place within it.

The third player—Petros in this case—is in a position to be entreated by the loser to hear his story and give credence (or at least respond, positively or negatively) to his complaints. Here, upon receiving the slightest response from Petros, Dhimitris continued, further making his case and restating his story. The dealer of the next hand, here Mikhalis, is the person responsible for moving the game along; he is reasonably in a position to be looking ahead to the next hand, having just put in his own money and now readying the cards. Therefore, he is the player most likely to have an interest in stopping the discussion, calling out, as Mikhalis did, "Come now! Are we playing or talking?"

It is interesting to note that although individual players see a familiarity with others' styles, gained over a history of other hands, as providing a distinct edge over the poker table, past claims about chance, such as those more than a few days old, play a very limited role in this setting. Or, perhaps more precisely, the relevant history of outcomes is so recent, encompassing most often only the evening's play, and thus brought so close to the unfolding present, that claims about this past effectively become claims about the immediate present and point much more to a coming future (and the possibilities of streaks continuing, for example), than a contested past. Rather than the use of history, then, one sees the use of the future, not only in claims about identity vis-à-vis chance but in constructions of that momentary reality itself. In this fleeting ordering of reality, a clear example of structuration, the principle of *gouri* plays a key role. The converse is of course also true, as a player who has been losing seeks to shake things up, to change the *gouri*, as Dhimitris did here. The brief passage that opens this chapter points to this kind of action as well, as Nondas tells the cards, "Wake up, bastard!"

The opening vignette of the Introduction provides a further example to emphasize how these references to *gouri* are embedded in local struggles such as those involved in running a business. The link between his failure at the card table, one that had left him in debt to the very man who had had a successful night as owner only a year before, and his failed investment in the dice table for this year was clear and was commented on by the players as they broke up for the evening and headed out into the night (many of them, as I later learned, to play *zaria* elsewhere). His immoderation in betting and bluffing that night mirrored, for them, his immoderation and ambition in setting up for a large number of customers on New Year's Eve. Such a railing against his misfortune as he performed, under the principles of *gouri*, was perhaps the only recourse by which he might bring about a change in his place in the world.[12]

Situating Chance

In how Chaniot gamblers understand the unfolding outcomes of their games, we see also how they understand the unfolding outcomes of their lives, and the links so quickly made by Greeks between gambling and social life more generally are made clear. A (dis)ordering of reality takes place in gaming contexts such as that of poker in Chania, one that arises between the participants (and other spectators) rather than solely within each actor's experience. Furthermore, the claims about indeterminacy that arise are made in a context structured by rules and conventions that nonetheless relies on chance to unfold. This characteristic of gambling, its aptness as an arena for structuration, also accounts for its potency as a metaphor for other spheres of everyday experience, themselves ostensibly but not ultimately structured as well and amid which individuals and institutions pit competing claims about accountability.

In this way gambling, though a part of everyday experience with significant consequences, nonetheless also provides a semibounded refraction of the precarious nature of everyday experience, a kind of distillation of a chanceful life into a seemingly more apprehensible form. Thus, at least a part of how gamblers in Chania confront indeterminacy lies in their attempts to position themselves or others vis-à-vis chance, using *gouri* and other tropes of chance to account for the unfolding of outcomes from one moment to the next and thereby negotiating an often ephemeral but nonetheless effective understanding of a local reality through this process of structuration. What is risked, then, over the gaming table, is what is exposed to the inspection of others: one's resources, one's intentions, and, above all, one's favorable or unfavorable position, however momentarily, in the present as it unfolds.

Notes

This chapter is adapted from an article titled "Fateful Misconceptions: Rethinking Paradigms of Chance among Gamblers in Crete," which appeared in *Social Analysis* 43 (1): 141–65.

1. It is of interest to note that one of the institutionalized risk systems that Giddens mentions is gambling, which he recognizes as universal but disregards as being a "relatively minor context" (1991, 117).

2. See also the work of James Carrier (1992). He considers Occidentalism in anthropological thought with reference to Mauss's *The Gift* (1990 [1925]) and specifically the problematic distinction of commodity versus gift societies, a discussion of reciprocity easily transferable to the equally problematic distinction of fate (nonmodern) versus risk (modern) societies. See also Douglas and Isherwood's *The World of Goods* (1978, 40) for a further example of this questionable approach discussed earlier.

3. See Becker (1997) for a somewhat similar exploration of meaning construction in the face of the unexpected, although the focus differs from mine in its emphasis on individual narrative.

4. Indeed, the two words may share a history: *Gouri* derives from the Turkish word *ugur,* which may be a cognate of the Latin *augur* (Herzfeld 1981). Note also that this model cannot simply be reduced to a notion of proximity, as personal practice and other events (one's favorite soccer team winning that day) can just as well be grounds for a claim of *gouri.*

5. By "poker *kafenio*" I mean a *kafenio* with card gambling where the most commonly played game is poker. At such a place other games (*tavli* [backgam-

mon] at side tables, *bilota* between two players) sometimes are played, but most often these are to pass the time while players wait for an opening at the current table or wait for enough players to make a new table.

6. To open the betting, a player must have at least a pair of kings or aces. The betting proceeds as in draw poker, with each player choosing to stay in (by putting in the same amount as the players still in) or fold. There are two rounds of betting, one before the players exchange their cards and one afterward. The ranking of the various poker hands is as follows (from highest to lowest): straight flush (*flous*), four of a kind, flush (*khroma*), full house (*foul*), three of a kind, straight (*kenta*), two pair, and one pair.

7. The cards themselves are plastic, not plastic-coated paper, and are very durable, even if their printing is not.

8. In a similar vein, stories of outwitting police officers, such as tricking them into eating stolen meat, are discussed by Herzfeld (1985, 220–22).

9. As will become clear later in this chapter, such a situation could easily have had a different result if my friend's luck had suddenly changed for the better.

10. This characterization of the *pekhtis* has many similarities with the image of the *mangas*, the dramatic, self-sufficient, antiestablishment figure associated with the musical subculture of *rebetiko* in 1920s urban Greece. See Cowan (1990, 173–75) for a concise account of this figure.

11. Indeed, these players often alluded to James Bond to get this idea across.

12. Similar links are made by those who play the state-sponsored lotteries and scratch ticket games between their success or failure in playing these games and their success in the other "national sport" of Greece, tax evasion; see chapter 4.

4   Playing the State's Game

It was a few weeks before New Year's Eve of 1994 at a bar in the newer part of town, and with a dice player named Stelios I was having the kind of conversation anthropologists favor: one-sided. Having just met him a few moments before, I was surprised at how quickly I was being led through Stelios's vision of his life as a gambler. I found myself subject to an intense display of personality because Stelios had, to put it mildly, an abundance of confidence in his gambling abilities. He also had great faith that his insights in this area were applicable to all aspects of social life, including business and romance. "I am a player [ime pekhtis]—not just a gambler—and a very good one," he said distinctly. Over the next few weeks I saw him regularly, and his persona was unflaggingly secure. Over the gaming table at a smoky gambling den in the old town, in a crowd of about twenty-five dice gamblers, Stelios continually took the spotlight, as well as a fair amount of money. At that time, apparently in his element, his dramatic confidence in his own abilities seemed well-placed.

It was late in January 1995 (just over a month later) that I came across Stelios once again; he was talking intently with two friends of mine, brothers who owned a hotel in the old harbor. He was quite agitated, barely saying hello as I approached before continuing his conversation. He was talking about the tax laws that had just gone into effect. It appeared that Stelios's two businesses (cafés on the beach just west of the city) had relied heavily on tax evasion, and he was now in doubt about how to proceed because he knew no way around the new laws. He cursed the new laws and the government, as had many others with whom I had spoken, and after only a few more words moved on. His manner was so uncharacteristic of him that I commented on it to Nikos, one of the hotel-owning brothers. Nikos smiled and said, "Do you remember when we talked about the biggest uncertainty in business here? The tax laws, remember? Stelios will have to learn a new game."

Nikos's comment points not only to the gamelike terms in which many Chaniots see their relationship with the Greek state (as apparently do Greeks elsewhere in the country; see, for example, Sutton 1997, 431n; and Herzfeld 1985) but also to another feature of that characterization, and that is the claim that the Greek state is inherently—and often maliciously and strategically—unpredictable. In contrast to the established academic literature, which has focused on how state processes routinize and homogenize, this view suggests that its unfathomable changeability can even be a source of state power. If this is the case, the further question becomes what the sources of this perceived unpredictability are and how they may collide with other kinds of uncertainties Chaniots (and Greeks in general) may confront, including both the broadly changeable nature of the global tourist market and the intimate and variable landscape of local public opinion. The degree to which state agents have success in promoting the playing of its "games" as unquestionable practice despite a public recognition of the state's own inconstancy may indicate a surprising amount of control over the arena of the uncertain on the part of the state.

Another example that the government's interests and judgments are considered suspect with regard to gambling and issues of chance and risk is well illustrated by an evening I spent in the village of Stilos, about twenty minutes by car outside of Chania. Late one afternoon I set out with a friend to see his village, located in a rich agricultural area about thirty kilometers from the city. With sizable amounts of well-irrigated citrus land below and hillsides of olive trees above, Stilos had a reputation as a financially well-off place, and it is notable that in 1994 its local school was still in full operation, unlike those in many other villages in Crete, which had lost much of their younger population to the city. My friend, Charis, lived in Chania but was still very active in the village (he carried many votes across party lines from the village in his ultimately unsuccessful attempt to run for political office with the coalition party of the left, *Sinaspismos*, in Chania), where his mother, brother, and nephews still lived, and there was a loud chorus of welcoming shouts as we entered one of the local coffeehouses early in the evening.

I was surprised to see a slot machine standing to one side because the few such gambling machines (as opposed to video games) that I had previously noticed had been in *kafenia* in Chania known for their gambling. Many of the regulars (as I later came to learn they were) were standing in front of it playing in a group. We walked over and watched as, before each pull of the handle, a few of those standing around each put in a 100-Dr coin. Each one who paid chose a line drawn in the windows across the dials—three across (one above, one in the middle, and one below) and two diagonally—each one indicating a line where a correct combination of the symbols of fruit on the dials would win as each successive coin activated one more line. Charis joined in and was soon engaged in almost managing the situation; as everyone played or watched he repeated who had which number and quickly recognized who had won (if anyone) each time, calling out his name in congratulations. Usually the first player to put in a coin each time then pulled the handle, but sometimes another took over. Others not playing nonetheless paid attention and gave comments. After a while, the group broke up, and everyone retired to chairs to chat and have coffee. It was then that I learned that the machine had been there for only two days, and everyone said that they were already growing bored with it.

An interesting discussion ensued, however, as I sat with the owner of the place along with Charis and the previous president of the village. It became clear that the *kafetzis,* the owner, had strong opinions about gambling machines, both the older manual slot machines such as this one (most often called *frutakia,* "little fruits") and newer ones that used a video screen for poker, blackjack, or slots. The owner, Stefanos, commented that the machine was legal, which required some explanation, because everyone knew that slot machines were illegal in Greece. Stefanos pointed out that the law said that games of skill were legal, to which everyone agreed, and then produced a photocopy of the legal decision where this was delineated. It turns out that throughout Greece the distributor of this game had succeeded in convincing the authorities that the game was legal because there was some degree of control over on which line one would bet. Everyone laughed at this notion—plainly no line was better than another, so it made no difference—and concluded that a lot of money must have changed hands for that decision to be bought. As for their increasing boredom with the machine, it later became clear that the locals did not use the machine individually, which is almost the only way I saw such machines played in the city. In Stilos, an ad hoc group played the machine, as described earlier, or did not. The only people who did play it singly, according to the regular patrons, were migrant agricultural workers, mostly from Albania; one of them now and then appeared in the coffeehouse, played for a few minutes, and then left.

To the locals such atomization of gambling was unattractive, for it pitted one against a machine rather than against other human beings, and this contrast is key for understanding the relationship between most forms of state gambling and illegal forms in the city itself.

The gambling activity examined in this chapter, the state-sponsored games, is in a similar way drastically different from the other forms of gambling I have considered. Rather than enacted within local networks, state gambling in Greece implicates both local relationships and those between locals, locales, and the Greek state. Tax evasion, by contrast, relied on collective forms of resistance to state surveillance, at least until tax law changed. This chapter thus explores how these dual transitions (in tax law and in state control over gambling) in a way mirror similar processes of increasing state control over arenas of indeterminacy.

A State of Caprice?

In January 1995 a change in the Greek municipal tax law went into effect in Chania that fundamentally shifted the way certain businesses were assessed taxes. The change was a shift away from a system that relied solely on a percentage of total receipts and toward a mixed system where not only these receipts but also the outdoor seating space of the establishment were incorporated into the calculation of the owed tax. The affected businesses were limited to designated "tourist" areas, and I focus here on how this change affected one such area, the old town of Chania, specifically focusing on the cafés, bars, and similar establishments therein. A microlevel examination of how ideas about tax evasion are articulated in Chania can illuminate not only how tax evasion is practiced and conceived throughout the Greek nation but also how the relationship between states and an illegal practice such as tax evasion is bound up not only in pattern and predictability but also in disorder and uncertainty.

To evade taxes under the previous system, owners relied on the complicity of customers (as I describe later in this chapter), but frequent random checks by the tax police, posing as customers, meant that these owners could confidently rely only on customers with whom they had gained some level of intimacy (Herzfeld 1997a). Still, many owners, under monetary pressure to cope with the often sporadic tourist business, often sought to evade these taxes even when dealing with unfamiliar customers. Although these techniques were still viable under the new system, the return from practicing them diminished, and owners struggled to adjust to the new situation, the "new game," as Nikos put it. I do not here discuss the specific finances of these businesses, not only because such information is (not surprisingly) closely guarded but also because my interest lies in another area: What does this mean for our conceptualization of the state itself? Long seen as the locus of structure and as heavily invested in maintaining order and predictability (a view that owes much of its social analytical lineage to Max Weber), recently conceptions of the state have broken new ground: Its reputedly monolithic character is now recognized as a strategic representation overlaying a complex and imperfect institution (March and Olsen 1989).

In one recent collection on the relationship between the state and criminality (particularly appropriate for the case at hand), this point was made directly: "Our general perspective emphasizes the incompleteness of formal states and the unlikelihood that they will entirely master their own and people's 'illegal' maneuvers" (Heyman 1999, 2). In the midst of this conceptual advance, how might we begin to understand how the state's "incompleteness" accounts for its apparent "capriciousness," its inconsistency across cases and the resultant unpredictable character of its actions? What is more, the use by state agents of what Christopher Hood (1996, 211) calls "contrived randomness" as part of their internal and external surveillance and control suggests that indeterminacy may not only arise from the complex interplay of the multiple agents that together constitute institutions like the state; it may also be an instrument in the arsenal of its agents, used strategically in certain circumstances. From this another question follows: If the state is also a locus of unpredictability, how might both its strategic use and its unintended emergence support existing relations of power? I argue that it is by examining both its techniques of tax law enforcement, which rely on randomness for their efficacy, and its extension of control over gambling, primarily through state-sponsored lotteries, that this feature of the state's imperfection can be brought to light, and its effect on the relationship between state and citizen can be explored.

This is doubly relevant given the increasing attention paid to the relationship between the state and criminality. Both changing tax policy and the rise of state-sponsored gambling, each shaped differently by the state agents responsible for their enforcement or marketing (note the fundamental difference revealed by this distinction alone), nonetheless can be seen as parallel processes from the point of view of policy mandates for the Greek state. This is most evident when considering the intense pressure brought to bear on Greece to recoup "lost" revenue by the European Union (Horn 1996), a demand that both of these initiatives purport to answer. Within academia as well, social scientists, particularly economists, have for years equated state-sponsored lotteries and other games with taxation. In their view, the games function as a regressive tax, with those from lower economic strata most likely to participate.

In Chania, remarkably, I found that Chaniots equated playing the games with tax *evasion,* an unexpected similarity from the point of view of economists but one that reveals much about the agonistic and indeterminate relationship between the individual, locale, and nation in Greece. Criminality, then, provides a particularly useful arena for reconsidering the state's coherence, as inconsistent or contradictory actions on the part of state agents are vulnerable to being labeled as "criminal" not only in cases where the applicability of formal law is clear but also in those where the actions simply do not accord with policy directives or established procedure. The sponsorship of gambling by nation-states is a particularly poignant example: Attempts to criminalize local and unregulated forms of gambling necessarily lie at odds, morally and logically, with efforts by other state representatives to market the state's games. The suggestion seems to be that only the state can authorize the taking of risks, a circumstance in which the state's apparent similarity to a casino (with its corresponding "house cut") opens it to obvious criticism, a vulnerability that Chaniots, at least, exploit frequently in their characterizations of the state.

In talking about tax evasion and tax policy many Chaniots invoke the idioms of sociality and indeterminacy. As I elaborate later in this chapter, Chaniots view the receipt-based aspect of tax assessment as encroaching in various ways on the practice of sociality—through, specifically, the demand that every exchange involve documentation. By sociality I mean here the learned practice of building and maintaining social relations through common activities (in this case, primarily commensal activities, including the practice of treating, an entrenched aspect of Greek social life and long the subject of Greek ethnography).[1] At the same time that Chaniots lament the connection between the state and sociality that receipts represent, they use techniques grounded in sociality to evade these taxes through the often tacit assent of particular customers with whom they have achieved some level of intimacy.

In these discussions about the state, the theme of indeterminacy arose in several ways, primarily through complaints about the capriciousness of the tax laws themselves. "They don't stay the same even for one hour!" another bar owner complained to me, citing this uncertainty as the single biggest obstacle new business owners must face and arguing that it was a greater "risk" than those typically associated with the tourist industry: the sometimes unfathomable, certainly uncontrollable, appearance or non-appearance of tourists in any given year. The combination of accusations of capriciousness by the very businesspeople who often take pride in navigating unpredictability in other domains and the strategic use of chance by the state itself (in random tax inspections and state-sponsored gambling) makes plain that the unpredictable is an arena of contest between state agents and local groups and individuals. By looking at these themes of sociality and indeterminacy and by considering the practice of state gambling as, in a way, a "mirroring practice" for tax evasion, one can begin to view this phenomenon in Greece as a further instance of the politics of contingency, instances wherein agents of institutions and other individuals and groups attempt to gain influence or "control over the perception of probabilities" (Asad 1993, 7, 17).

The two sources of indeterminacy with which I am concerned here are the social and an aspect of the formal that I call the systemic. In the former, the issue of never knowing others' opinions with certainty takes center stage, and actors must rely on social acumen in their taking of risks that depend on guessing at others' views. The key point is that this ability to confront the inherently chanceful quality of individual opinion is of a different type than that involved in confronting broadly stochastic unpredictabilities. The latter kind is a kind of formal indeterminacy, a product of a set of factors so complex as to preclude prediction. This type has been made popularly familiar through the attention recently garnered by chaos theory. The classic examples of pure contingency—a dice rolling or a butterfly flapping its wings to change global weather or the length of Cleopatra's nose—are indeterminate precisely because they are the result of a hypercomplex set of factors. By systemic indeterminacy (as an aspect of formal indeterminacy) I mean in particular the unpredictability of the large-scale systems that are the product of concerted human effort and rationalized knowledge (in the Weberian sense), whether those systems are economic, political, or of other kinds. To refer to this type as systemic indeterminacy underscores how these human institutions, such as the one that concerns us here, can be themselves the locus of unpredictability in this chaotic way. Sally Falk Moore (1978, 39) calls attention to this feature of institutions in her suggestion that indeterminacy must be accounted for in examinations of the tensions between "the pressure toward establishing and maintaining order and regularity, and the underlying circumstance [of] counteractivities, discontinuities, variety, and complexity [that] make[s] social life inherently unsuited to social ordering." And just as a demonstrated ability to engage social indeterminacy effectively can result in social gain, the ability to confront systemic indeterminacy with élan can pay off in terms of social standing as well (an apt phrase for this, though from a different context, is "social grace," used by James Faubion 1993, 5). But again, at least in Greece, these abilities are distinct, a point underscored to me by the characterization of a friend and contact of mine, who was socially adept, by his younger brothers, who ran their jointly owned hotel (his story is discussed at length in chapter 6). They said he "had no head" (*"dhen ikhe nou"*) for managing a tourist business and portrayed his skills as effective only for village life of the past (they thus placed him out of place *and* time; notably this is an example of a denial of coevalness *within* a local context [cf. Fabian 1983]).

This chapter thus takes as its inspiration three sources. Asad's (1993, 7, 17) cogent injunction to pay attention to how authorities and experts may seek to shape the perception of uncertainties and the interpretation of outcomes provides the backdrop for this inquiry.[2] Second, the work by Heyman and others in drawing attention to both the complex nature of the state itself (partially influenced by the "new institutionalism," see March and Olsen 1989) and to its interwoven relationship with illegal practices informs the conceptualization of the state throughout this chapter. Third, Hood's recognition of the strategic use of randomness by institutions seeking to control both workers and customers further complicates the picture. In what follows I draw further together these two new threads of thought about the state (its complexity or indeterminacy and its strategic use of chance) through a consideration of tax evasion and state-sponsored gambling participation in Chania. In this account there also emerges a tension between these two sources of indeterminacy as the skills drawn on to navigate social indeterminacy with efficacy collide with attempts by state agents to enforce policy, practices that instead pit individual Chaniots against a state apparatus that is imperfect yet not to be ignored.

Taxing Techniques

The prevalence of the practice of tax evasion has escaped few people's attention in Greece. The phrase most commonly heard, in Chania at least, in conjunction with the practice is "national sport" (*ethniko pekhnidhi*), and it is with this "sport" and how people make sense of it that I am concerned. The problem of tax evasion in any nation-state points to a complex relationship between the individual and the state. When a pattern or notion of contest, such as in Greece, permeates how relationships are represented, both between the individual and the state and between individuals and groups, what are the available strategies of a state wishing to recoup "lost" revenue? When tax revenue is lost in this way as a result of local strategies of (seemingly) collective resistance, how can different formulations of the tax system subvert them? In a similar way, the Greek state has increasingly attempted to gain revenue from the activity of gambling, the illegal forms of which evade the state's attempts to profit from commercial activity. The number and variety of Greece's state-sponsored games have exploded in the postwar period to recoup this revenue. How does this trend reflect a similar process of the subversion of local forms of sociality—and the engagement of social indeterminacy that characterizes them—in favor of gambling that pits individual Greeks against the state in an atomized fashion?

The tax police in charge of enforcing the tax laws among service establishments in Chania primarily use a couple of different strategic practices to combat tax evasion (*forodhiafiyi*). These practices for the most part target attempts to evade reporting purchases accurately on the establishment's receipts, and thus have not changed substantially with the new tax law (but new techniques to enforce the flat rate portion of the tax for service and tourist businesses are described later in this chapter). One of these practices used to curb receipt-based tax evasion, is spot checks, the sudden, ideally unannounced (from the tax agency's point of view) arrival of tax inspectors who declare themselves and proceed to check every receipt on each customer's table. If a table does not have a receipt, or if the receipt does not reflect the food and drink purchases, a stiff fine is levied on the owner.

In many cases, however, business owners in Chania hear news of the tax inspectors, who usually target a particular part of the tourist-filled old city or a nearby waterfront area, checking a number of businesses within a several-block radius. Word quickly spreads among owners through phone calls, delivery people, and employees. One of the latter (often a son, daughter, or other younger relative of the owner) may head off to take a walk, just as the police arrive, to spread the word. In addition, because the tax inspectors in these checks are locals, they may forewarn those with whom they have ties of friendship, patronage, or kinship. In one such case I encountered, a business owner received a morning phone call from his wife informing him that her friend—a neighbor and the tax inspector's wife—had mentioned to her when they met in the street that her husband expected to be in that part of the city that day. Another well-known instance concerns one of the most notorious illegal gamblers in Chania, who also happened to have a high-profile position with the city. Well-placed as he was, and also a regular customer at many of the old town's gambling dens—which during the summer as "cafés" had tourist business—it often became difficult for tax inspectors to catch any of these places in violation. One can see that the links across the domains of public office, private business, and illegal activity are powerful and more common than is often publicly acknowledged (because, naturally, those who benefit do not want to call attention to them).

The other primary enforcement procedure the tax police use is random, undercover checks, in which tax inspectors from other areas come to a city with which they are not familiar to pose as customers and catch owners in the act of neglecting receipts or giving false or old ones. Here local tax inspectors have little chance to notify kin and cohort because the disguised tax inspectors are free to move as they will about the area. Hood (1996, 211, 213) calls this "contrived randomness," which he likens to a slot machine ("fruit-machine"; note the links to gambling even here). He continues, characterizing it as follows:

> In the "fruit-machine" style of bureaucracy, division of authority (for example separation of payment from authorization and "multiple-key" operations), linked with limited tenure, rotation of staff to avoid overfamiliarity with clients, semi-random postings of employees to countries or cities other than those in which they were born and brought up, together with unannounced random (and perhaps undetectable) checks, reduces the motives and opportunity for anti-system cooperation. Probably it is not necessary for such operations to be truly random in a strict statistical sense, provided they are widely *believed* to be random by those affected. (1996, 213)

Both of these procedures of enforcement are instances of contrived randomness in that they involve the use of random timing to achieve a degree of control. As with the first practice, there are ways to guard against this unpredictable form of surveillance as well, however, and this is by cultivating social intimacy with one's customers, thus pitting one's ability to hazard the vagaries of trusting others against the deployment of randomness by state agents.

Most service businesses (cafés, bars, coffeehouses, restaurants) in the "tourist" section (primarily the old town) rely to some extent on local business throughout the year, that is, other Chaniots who frequent these places when they take their evening stroll along the harbor, for example, or (especially among the youth of the city) when going out to meet friends. (Santrivani Square, desribed in chapter 1, is just such a place.) This local business then becomes the primary business during the off season. The weather in Crete aids this effort by allowing outdoor seating much of the year. Supplemented by the use of portable outside kerosene heaters by some businesses, Chaniots can enjoy an afternoon coffee by the harbor throughout the year and even late into the evening in winter. As a result, many of these businesses can rely on the complicity of their local regulars in their neglect of receipts. There are two primary techniques for evading the receipt-based portion of the tax, both of course used exclusively (and by some, like Stelios, extensively) before the system changed.

The first technique is simply not to give a receipt for the customer's purchase, whether it be a drink, a sandwich, or the like. This form of tax evasion overlaps in practice with acts of sociality, as it is common for a customer who is a good friend or frequent regular to order something and then only later, when seeking to pay for it, be told that it was the treat (*kerasi*) of the owner or server. It was particularly annoying to one couple that I knew, who owned a very popular beerhouse in the old town, that they were "not allowed" even to treat their friends at their own establishment. They both railed extensively at the government for its intrusion into their practices of sociality. It was a reliable indication for me, as a foreign-born researcher, that I had passed to a deeper level of intimacy with a café owner when I stopped having receipts placed on my table. On the rare days when I again received a receipt (often with a quick apology by the owner) it was a clear sign that the tax inspectors were about. To know one's customer well enough to guess confidently that they will not spread word of tax evasion relied on a subtle assessment of the customer's attitudes and trustworthiness, the skillful playing of a game (engaging social indeterminacy) quite different from that played with the tax system itself.

This first type of tax evasion was used only with intimates because of the obviousness to the customer. However, the second common tax evasion technique could be tried, with some risk, with any customer, and was favored by businesses that relied on tax evasion extensively (such as Stelios). The method is to give an old (from earlier in the day) or falsely under-cost receipt, often tucked under an ashtray or curled into a shot glass to keep it from being blown away by the wind. This technique has the advantage of appearing, to a casual visual check, to accord with the law. Because many menu items at cafés have the same price, it is often difficult, if not impossible, to be sure that the receipt does not represent the product at hand. Furthermore, because Chaniots often spend more than half a day at a waterfront café in the old town (before their shift at work begins, for example), who is to say that the time stamped on the receipt is so implausible? In addition, because the text portion of the receipts is in Greek, tourists could in most cases be assumed not to be able to read the receipt accurately anyway. Instead, most asked a waiter to pay and then, after he arrived and checked the receipt, relied on the waiter's statement of the total. This type of tax evasion is particularly risky when nonlocal tax inspectors are about. The pressure to reduce taxes when the tourist business has been spotty can be intense, and Stelios was not alone in seeking to maximize unrecorded sales. Thus, many owners felt compelled to make careful guesses about Greek-speaking strangers, noting clues such as accent, age, clothing, attitude, and amiability in attempting to spot an undercover inspector.

Such techniques of tax evasion made use of business owners' social facility, their ability to engage social indeterminacy with confidence and success. In berating the Greek state for demanding the recording of transactions these owners were not merely lamenting the intrusion of state business into sociality but were also signaling how such regulation attacked the very arena used in the struggle to evade taxes. The use of systemic indeterminacy, in this case contrived randomness specifically, on the part of state agents countered this local reliance on social indeterminacy, raising the stakes of the contest by making any social interaction between an owner and customer a potential moment of exposure. The change in the law, which shifted the terms of the issue in a fundamental fashion, brought with it a new combination of sources of indeterminacy and called for a new means of counteracting them on the part of owners. I had the good fortune to see one of these instances unfold.

In May 2000, during a brief trip to Chania, I was interviewing one of the city's most successful entrepreneurs, Nektarios, who had opened a café in the old town on the water that for a time was the talk of the city and continued to have good business. It was early in the day, and the just-risen sun shone brightly in our eyes, reflecting off the water on the eastern side of the promontory on which the old town rests. Most of the cafés along this street, nearly all of which had sprung up in the wake of Nektarios's café's success (this area had previously not been commercially developed), were still closed, and their outdoor chairs were folded up, or drawn close to the small tables, and the umbrellas were furled. Nektarios had suggested we meet early because he liked to be at the local center for Greek stock market trading as soon as it opened (he was widely known as a substantial local player of the market). As we spoke, a tax police officer strolled by, and Nektarios was immediately anxious. "Just a moment," he said quickly, as he rose from his chair to step down to the street level and look around. Soon he was engaged in an animated discussion with the police officer. Arriving at the street myself, I looked around and saw the cause for concern: A young man dressed in white painter's clothes, using a paint roller on a pole, was slowly painting a white line along street, marking the edge of the cafés' seating areas. (The cafés used space not only on the sidewalks that ran along the seawall but also on both sides of the street itself, allowing only enough space for one traffic lane on the one-way street.)

The purpose of the line was not primarily for keeping the tables and chairs out of the car lane, however. I had seen the line elsewhere during the previous couple of days, drawn around the outdoor seating areas of other cafés in the pedestrian-only parts of the old town. It was for tax purposes—a way for the local tax inspectors to inscribe the appropriate boundaries on each of the businesses. Previously, they had used only a small can of spray paint, of a neutral color, to mark an "L" at the corners of the seating area; now, however, the paint was white and was rolled on heavily, in a strip about six inches wide. I was told by another business owner that marking the area so obviously served a couple of purposes. On one hand, it helped adjudicate disputes between adjacent businesses over potentially ambiguous space. It also was an attempt by the tax police to keep business within the space allocated to each owner, he said. "But who knows," he continued, "one inspector cares, the next does not." Local tax police officials, I should mention, strenuously resisted my attempts at formal and informal interviews. It is not clear whether they objected to how my work might locally emphasize them as state agents or whether it might have drawn the attention of their superiors, itself an example of how the unpredictable (in this case, the consequences of my work) can exert power. Another possibility that is consistent with other portrayals of Greek bureaucracy (if not bureaucracy generally) is that the refusals were part of a strategy of deflecting responsibility, as Herzfeld (1992) discusses extensively.

In the bright morning sun, Nektarios was pointing and, with a smile ever on his face, gently questioning the officer about the direction the lines were heading as the painter approached (he was about two businesses away at this point). "You know, of course, the road makes several very slight turns along here," he said, "Why should the lines stay so straight?" As they continued, with Nektarios pointing here and there, the painter took a break while watching them, sitting on the curb and smoking a cigarette as Nektarios and the officer conversed. Nektarios was clearly concerned that if the lines continued straight down the street toward his café, his business would end up with an overlarge area of marked-off space, one that did not fit his careful layout of just so many tables and so many chairs. Knowing that to pay taxes on such wasted space would be expensive, he lobbied to ensure that the painter would make slight corrections to the line as he continued. The officer, for his part, was noncommittal, but the painter heard each word, and later when I saw the finished lines they ran right up to the back feet of Nektarios' chairs, which were drawn in close to his tables. Of course, when used the chairs would be pulled back and cross the line, but this did not concern Nektarios. "The important thing," he said to me, "is that that is *their* line. They can't blame me if they drew it so close [to the tables]." He chuckled and smiled broadly. "You know," he continued, "they came to do it this early because they thought no one would be here." Indeed, Nektarios was the only owner or other worker who had yet arrived. "But by coming now and following the street like I said they draw the lines very narrowly; we've all saved a little today."

Again, we see the strategic use of the unpredictable here, but in a case where it led to unintended consequences (Giddens 1984). Nektarios was there that early only by chance (to meet me) and would not otherwise have had an opportunity to plead his case. Also, by seeking to avoid contact with shop owners, the tax police were left to apply their boundaries in the absence of customers, leading to an inability to assess accurately the space as used. In other areas of the old town, the lines were drawn during business hours and reflected the expansion of such space, costing those owners more. Does the combination of Nektarios's appeal and this misapplication add up to tax evasion? Or does it instead reveal that the imperfect state, even while trying to make use of indeterminacy, can just as well be caught up in yet another inconsistency? In any case, perhaps the deepest irony here is that the shift of some of the assessment to a flat-rate system led the municipal tax office to seek to clarify visibly the extent of these concrete spaces. Yet at the same time, to demarcate them necessarily placed tax officials and owners together in a different way than before, as it did for Nektarios—a way that opened the door for the reading of others that marked a social virtuoso. His own ability to plead his case gently while also succeeding in causing enough confusion that the painter stopped until his case was heard attests to his mastery in the domain of social indeterminacy.

Playing the State's Game

Like practices of tax evasion, the state-sponsored games played in Chania and elsewhere in Greece call to the fore the often problematic relationship between Greek citizens and the Greek state. The most visibly recognizable difference between how these state-sponsored games are played in Chania and how other, illegal ones are played, is the state-sponsored games' relative isolation. Card games, played in card-playing clubs, homes, and coffeehouses; dice gambling, discoverable only in hidden and temporary places; and backgammon, found nearly everywhere, all involve the social scrutiny of individuals, either publicly or among a circumscribed group, and so in all of these games, albeit in different ways, the players are to a certain extent on display.

The playing of state games, by contrast, is almost completely removed from sociality and the observation of others, as it is played almost exclusively on an individual basis in lottery shops. What is more, nearly every state game player with whom I spoke reported that the activity of purchasing Lotto, Pro-To, or Ksisto tickets was done as an errand while individually moving about Chania, claims supported by observations I made in the lottery shops. Customers arrived singly in nearly every case, and, after sometimes giving a brief greeting to the shop owner or worker (usually little more than a nod), they grabbed some blank game forms and moved to the small tables or counters along the walls to fill them out. When ready, the forms were fed into the shop's computerized reader (of a type familiar in many countries with extensive state-sponsored gambling, such as the United States) and official tickets printed out, while the money changed hands. After a brief goodbye (or none at all), the transaction was complete.

Despite (or perhaps because of) this lack of sociality in the lottery shops, they have some of the most colorful storefronts in Chania. Multicolored, large letters proclaim "LOTTO" accompanied by an image of a soccer ball (with a "1," a "2," and an "x" in three of its white spaces) advertising the soccer pool game Pro-Po. Each place is independently owned (in 1995 there were about sixty in the prefecture, about thirty in the city proper), the owner buying from the state the right (as a franchise) to market and sell the state games.

Standing in one of the larger lottery shops in the city, I saw immediately a kind of history in the place, as there were many older signs, brown with age, advertising the longer-running games, such as the lotteries (*lahia*) and Pro-Po. These contrasted with the posters in the windows that were obviously new, such as those for the scratch ticket game, Ksisto. Primary colors dominated throughout, with a bright yellow the most common. The store windows, covered with signs and posters, spanned the entire front wall of the shop and had a slightly disproportionate number of posters and advertisements for Lotto. One such advertisement read, "Lotto, it metes out millions" (*"Lotto, mirazi ekatomiria"*), where the concept of fate is invoked here in its verb form, meaning "to deal" or "to mete out." This poster provides a first clue as to how the state markets its games and along with them emphasizes a trope of accountability. The windows also featured signs with the most recent Lotto and Pro-To results.

Inside, the bright white walls and bright posters did not overcome a kind of uncared-for bleakness. The walls had mostly framed objects, including pictures of soccer games, maps showing the locations of the professional soccer teams of Greece and Italy, and documents with places for many Lotto and Pro-To numbers (the numbers written on the glass with washable marker). The primary need of customers is to have a space to fill out their forms quickly, and high tables built into the walls and simple (press-board and white laminate) chairs and desks, all of them covered with inexpensive pens, served this purpose. Stickers for the various games covered the main desk, on which sat the reading machine and behind which sat the clerk.

There was also a television there, either for the employees to pass the time or for players to watch the results of the games as they became available. Hanging from a small stand near the television were a number of keychains, each made of clear plastic and filled with very small balls that could be made to rest in depressions numbered from one to forty-nine. These were old (from about ten years earlier) complimentary items

A state lottery shop. (Author's collections)

that customers could use to choose Lotto numbers randomly. "Do people use these any more?" I asked Manolis, the clerk. "Sometimes, yes, but now the computer can choose numbers for you and people can do it that way. But most of them always play the same numbers, so what do they need that for?"

In the shops, customers fill out their choices of numbers (or teams, for Pro-Po, the soccer pool, but see later in this chapter) on small cards that are then run through a reading machine, which records the bets. The results for all of the games are announced on television, printed in local and national newspapers, and posted in the windows of the shops. These postings, along with the numerous advertisements for the various games, nearly cover the large-paned windows of the lottery shops.

The games themselves are, as mentioned, of three types: lotteries (including both Lotto and Pro-To—newer games—and the older *lahia*), the soccer pool (Pro-Po), and the instant-win scratch ticket games.[3] There are four forms of *lahio* in Greece run by the government in addition to Lotto and Pro-To. As mentioned earlier, *lahia* are lotteries in which each person has a set of numbers exclusively. The oldest, the Laiko, is played every week; recently (about five years ago) the government started rolling over jackpots that were not won each week into the next week's prize rather than returning the unclaimed money back to the state. Another form of *lahio* is called the Kratiko. This lottery works like an elimination tournament. Each week if one's number is listed one wins a little money, but more importantly one can enter the next week's drawing. Over the course of six months the winners are slowly reduced until only one is left, who may win a billion or more drachmas (about US$4 million). The final form of *lahio* is played only once a year, the Protokhroniatiko, a game "for the new year."

Scratch ticket games are also very similar to those seen in the United States, and in fact are manufactured there (with Greek-designed printing). There are usually about three or four different kinds of cards at any time in Greece, each one with a particular theme to the game, such as basketball or another sport. There is not much to playing them, however, as one merely scratches off some or all of the card to reveal whether one has won; there are of course no clues to determining which cards are winners. The cards are such that it is easy and inexpensive to change their printing, so new themes come out roughly every three months.

Pro-Po, the soccer pool game, is played by indicating, for each of the thirteen matches listed each week (selected from various local and other leagues) one of three options. One marks a "1" by a match to indicate that the home team will win, a "2" to indicate that the visiting team will win, or an "x" to indicate a tie. The games are normally played every Sunday, and the more of the outcomes one predicts correctly, and the fewer other players who do so, the more money one wins. It is thus the only state-sponsored game in which skill plays a role, although it is extremely difficult to follow soccer closely enough to be familiar with all of the teams playing in a given week because the games are drawn from a wide variety of leagues, primarily from Europe but always with a few from further afield. The game is played mostly by men (up to 95 percent, according to the estimates I received from *praktorio* operators); many of my male gambling friends spoke about having played it even if they did not generally play other games. However, most of them had finally quit, one of them calling it "a game of my youth" because "I used to be crazy for soccer. I knew everything. But you know something? Even when I won, I won very little because of all the other players who also chose correctly each week."

Pro-Po is an important and informative exception to the pattern of state gambling as monadic. Because it is a pool, all the players with the highest number of correct predictions split the prize money. Thus, unlike the other games, making guesses about the opinions of other players (such as whether a particular assumption about a team is widespread, and then whether this is justified) is a central aspect of the game. This element of social indeterminacy is so central as to lead some players with whom I spoke to take chances intentionally as they sought out obscure information about participating teams that lay outside the popular European league venues to maximize their profit should their long shots come in.

There is also a marked difference in the way Pro-Po is played. Instead of individuals stopping to fill out their cards at the local lottery shop alone, most Pro-Po players (for the most part young men) pore over soccer publications and the sport sections of Greek newspapers while having a coffee during a break at their place of work. This is also an occasion for trusted intimates to be consulted; a good friend once asked me for my best prediction about the upcoming U.S.–South Africa international friendly match, discounting my claims about a lack of knowledge of the sport. It is a common sight in the old town of Chania to see pairs of hunched-over figures, sitting at the small tables of the *stekia* (hangouts) of the old city, reading, calling on their cell phones, and scribbling on a new form in yet another attempt to complete their Pro-Po ticket.

However, Pro-Po appeals to a limited range of customers and capitalizes on the worldwide popularity of soccer among primarily a certain age group and gender. For similar reasons it is also a profitable game because of the sheer volume of matches played in organized leagues around the world, allowing the state lottery authority to concoct some obscure combinations of games, ensuring through this appeal to systemic indeterminacy a truly difficult game, one which for which there is no secret trick or method. Only the investment of enormous amounts of time can even begin to turn the odds in a player's favor, and this is then undercut by diminishing returns the more players win any given week. Pro-Po, though still revealing the interplay of the two sources of indeterminacy that concern me here, connects the Greek state to its citizens in a different way than its more traditional lotteries. With these, by contrast, there is only the contingency that arises from the distribution of numbers itself, layered over which are the marketing efforts, which battle to establish the meaning of playing and winning them according to a discourse of fate. In the marketing of Pro-Po, by contrast, the rhetoric of fate is completely absent, and instead the posters and television ads highlight the excitement of the sport itself, putting forth participation in Pro-Po as an enhancement of an experience to which the player has already committed.

What, then, does the atomization of state game participation reveal about the ways in which chance is engaged in the context of state-controlled games? Following Talal Asad's provocative suggestion about the deployment of power and control over the perception of probabilities (an idea also considered by Urla 1993), I suggest that the recent expansion of Greek state control over gambling has important implications for how Chaniots come to view contingency. Although the stated aim of the new casinos and games was to recover much of the tax revenue lost to the illegal gambling business throughout Greece (conservatively estimated to be about 2 billion Dr, or roughly US$8 million each year; Horn 1996), in providing the opportunity to control more and more the arenas of gambling the initiative gives the government the opportunity to exert an increasing amount of influence over how risk and chance are *talked about.* The control exerted by nation-states and corporations over the spaces of gambling through the increasingly popular state games and casinos constitutes a "colonization of the future" (Giddens 1991, 125), a means by which agents of these institutions can influence and shape attitudes toward the future and, more fundamentally, toward the indeterminacy of social life. These influences are to be found as much in the marketing of the games as anywhere else: One poster for Lotto, the largest Greek lottery, proclaimed, "It puts your fate in your hands!" Furthermore, the parallel shift away from sociality toward monadic participation both in state gambling and in tax policy changes entails a shift from the engagement of risks based on the social reading of others and toward risk taking under the auspices of the state apparatus.

If sociality is the terms in which the game of tax evasion is played for certain businesses in Chania, what are the terms of the game when it comes to state-sponsored gambling? To read from the advertisements at the lottery shops, the answer is *mira*, fate, a regular feature of much writing about Greece but a trope nearly absent from the discourse of most Chaniot gamblers in the context of the local and illegal forms of gambling. But fate in the context of the state games reappears in their marketing continually, and it is not simply determinative in the narrow sense of fatalism. "Your fate is in your hands!" another poster for Lotto cries, neatly invoking a powerful and inevitable destiny while making it paradoxically dependent on one's action to take part in the lottery. The state's lottery marketers thus colonize an approach toward contingency, saying, chillingly, that to have a chance at your destiny you must play the state's game. And this point of view is one that many players of other (illegal) games cited as the reason for their avoidance of the state games. "Why do they believe the lies?" implored one to me in a heated discussion about the topic. "Only the state wins." This sentiment was repeated over and over (much like the frequently heard view on casinos, "Only the house [casino] wins").

No Chaniot I came to know spent more every day on state games than Khronis, a jeweler who had owned a shop by the picturesque old harbor for almost seven years. Whenever I went by to see him, scratch tickets and lottery cards littered the space behind the display cases, with stacks of winning tickets (with small pay-offs) here and there and others, losing cards, torn up and tossed about. Khronis had been playing for about four years when I met him in 1994 and at first told me that he bet about 10,000 Dr (about US$40) a week. As we spoke however, it became clear that Khronis bet closer to 30,000 Dr (about US$120) each week on state games, playing all of them in roughly equal measure. He has won on several occasions, once winning 500,000 Dr (about US$2,000) at Lotto. He also plays all the *lahia* and has won twice, once 400,000 Dr (US$1,600), the other for 500,000 Dr (US$2,000). Ksisto, the scratch ticket game that had only been around for a couple of years when we met, he plays all the time, but he had not won anything yet when last we spoke. Also, and significantly, Khronis was not a player of illegal games, except on New Year's Eve, when he said that he played a little blackjack with family and friends.

When I asked why he plays, Khronis told me that ever since he won at Lotto, which happened shortly after he began playing, he had played continuously, and he suggested that his two other wins were an indication that, at least as far as the state games were concerned, he wins. "But what about all of the other money of yours that the state has taken from you [in playing the games]?" I asked. "That's my taxes," he replied, laughing, "since I don't pay any the normal way!" Between this account and that of Stelios earlier, we see the quick connection made by many Chaniots between the state-sponsored games and the practice of tax evasion. In both cases, the agonistic relationship is paramount.

As a result of this relationship, a significant number of Chaniots with whom I spoke tersely rejected state forms of gambling, characterizing them as means of oppression. One such man argued that the games provided the state with a "pressure valve" by which to let off the steam of the accumulated anger of the Greek people, and this statement is an example of how Chaniots themselves not only are suspicious of the state in its desire to take money away from citizens but may also see the threat as lying at a deeper, more alarming level. In this view, the games may provide the government with a way to manage resistant discourses, defining the rules of the game within which the populace has little room to maneuver. The actions of those who refused to play state-sponsored games recall Simone de Beauvoir's characterization of the position of a woman under male authority: "Out of respect for the whole system of accepted principles she should agree; if she refuses, she rejects the entire system. But she cannot venture to go so far; she lacks the means to reconstruct society in different form. Halfway between revolt and slavery, she resigns herself reluctantly. . . . [S]he refuses to play the game because she knows the dice are loaded" (Beauvoir 1952, 612).

Those who play the games, such as Khronis, see no contradiction between their desire to use deceit against the state in tax evasion and their practice of playing the games. They claim that the games provide a different kind of opportunity to cheat or outwit the state, to reverse the state's practice of stealing from citizens through tax collection, a view that pits the position of the player vis-à-vis chance directly against the position of the state, the "winner" of which is revealed, momentarily, in the result of each game the player plays and over time. Thus, Khronis saw his fortunate wins in the past as an indication that in his own struggle against the state he had the upper hand, a conviction about which I imagine the authorities of the national lotteries may have been pleased to hear, and this conviction continued through the end of my time in Chania, by which point more than a year had passed since his last win of more than a few hundred drachmas.

As for the prevalence of the concept of fate in the marketing of state games, it was a favorite topic of derision from many Chaniot gamblers who also played other games. Upon the mention of the advertisements, one gambler exclaimed to me, "Do you know what *mira* [fate] means? It means you close your eyes! Then you can't do anything. You don't know anything!" The theme of visibility is informative here because to many gamblers in Chania fate implies not only the inability to influence one's fortunes but also the inability to *apprehend* them, to read any indications of one's place amid chance (the key skill in *tavli*, as discussed in chapter 2). In particular, the advertisement suggesting that in state games one had the opportunity to influence one's fate brought further derision from the gamblers, directed toward both the state itself, for insulting them with the idea that playing the games was a "good risk," and toward those who played them excessively.

The lack of an appeal to the trope of fate among Chaniots, and Chaniot gamblers in particular, and its simultaneous ubiquity in state advertising for the lotteries, raises questions about the status of a concept with such a long history in Greek ethnography, as discussed in the Introduction. It may be more useful, then, to see fate as one means of accounting for the unexpected, deployed variously even within Greece and often bound up in power relations. This allows us to reinterpret the apparent incongruity in Chania above as instead an instance of the politics of contingency, where ways of interpreting indeterminacy (as a game where skill counts most, as part of an already written fate) compete in the flow of uncertain experience. The position of the gamblers and others in Chania who reject fate as a determinant of fortune are not offering an explicit counterdiscourse; instead, they navigate the shifting of state policy, economic market, and social opinion with an attitude that puts the emphasis on practically engaging these indeterminacies while still criticizing the government for its inconsistency.

Hegemonic Disorder

The identification of the practices and policies of the state with processes of atomization that run counter to local ties is an important claim but not a novel one. What is novel in the foregoing discussion is the recognition of both the state's use of randomness, both intended and unintended, and its influence over the perception of probabilities in such a way as to shift the terms of the engagement of chance. By appealing to systemic indeterminacy in a contrived sense in both new tax policy and expanded state gambling, agents of the Greek state place themselves implicitly and explicitly against the techniques of engaging social indeterminacy that are often used in concert by Greek citizens. Accustomed as we may be to viewing state practices as valorizing pattern and order, we may have become blind as to how that state may find unpredictability to be a source of power, whether in its reputed or actual capriciousness or in its ability, through the politics of contingency, to dictate the terms on which the future and its uncertainty are understood.

As in any consideration of policy enforcement (or marketing) in the nation-state, the issue of hegemony is recurrent, and it runs like a thread implicitly through much of the foregoing discussion. From Khronis's insistence that in his playing of the state's game he was ahead, if not materially, to Nikos's portrayal of Stelios's predicament and solution (that he learn a new game), Chaniots in the midst of tax policy changes and state game profusion grappled primarily with whether and how to play the state's game in one form versus another rather than whether to play it at all. Yet the view of the state as a complex and imperfect institution that informs this essay forces us to reevaluate the ability of the state to dominate its citizens' worldviews to the degree that a casual treatment of hegemony would suggest. Instead, in combination with the ethnographic material in this chapter, a revised view of the state leads to a picture of struggles between locals and state agents as full of chance meetings, inconsistent treatment, colliding (and at times self-defeating) strategies, and unintended consequences. Still, it must be admitted that agents of the state may benefit from a government's reputation for inconsistency and capriciousness. In this respect, unpredictability may be a source of state power, but it is an unwieldy weapon, one that nearly as often may damage its owner's interests, as in Nektarios's ability to capitalize on a situation initially designed to aid the tax police.

The more alarming implication of this interplay lies in the successful expansion of state-sponsored gambling in Greece, where it appears that the state's attempt to supplant engagements of indeterminacy among relative social intimates (in illegal forms of gambling) has had some success among those, such as Khronis, who have shifted their agonistic engagement of chance from their own cohort to the state. Having a chance at one's destiny, for more and more Chaniots, involves regularly playing the state lotteries, it seems. How can the state be both a locus of uncertainty and the trusted and final arbiter of high-stakes games of chance? Although discourses criticizing either the state's capriciousness or its status as a "casino" are prevalent in Chania, the remarkable thing is that they are rarely brought together. That focused discussion of this incongruity appears only in sporadic castigations of the state by individuals (such as in that of the Chaniot who saw the games as part of a pressure cooker–style management of resistance) attests to a hegemonic acceptance of the normal course of things in the way that Gardiner describes (1992, 183): "Hegemony does not simply correspond to a formal and coherent 'ideological' system because it submits largely unconscious and taken-for-granted meanings, values, and practices—that is, culture itself—to asymmetrical relations of power." As Heyman (1999, 7) puts it, "The effectiveness of hegemony depends on the skill with which people's common sense can be drawn upon to support the perception of the naturalness and inevitability of the existing state of affairs."

John Borneman (1992, 315) writes that "ideal unity in the state is all about equal life chances," and this statement echoes Asad's observations in placing the issues of the future and unpredictability at the core of nation-states' claims to legitimacy. The situation in Chania suggests that local business owners, customers, and state agents must all contend with, on one hand, the inherent complexity of the state itself, which leads often to inconsistent treatment across cases, and, on the other, the interplay between both social and systemic indeterminacy, deployed as they are by both agents and businesspeople to navigate an always uncertain economic and political landscape. The status of the state as the preeminent player in all these cases remains unquestioned because its various agents have vast resources both for the broad dissemination of marketing campaigns and for extensive surveillance practices. However, in local practice the ability to evade and otherwise avoid state control can vary to such a great extent that one might be tempted to question the true extent of state power. The key, however, is that although in small instances owners such as Nektarios (and players such as Khronis, perhaps) can win in ways and with frequency that can be surprising, in the end it is the state's game that they are most often playing.[4]

Notes

1. See Herzfeld (1985), Dubisch (1986), Cowan (1990), and Loizos and Papataxiarchis (1991).

2. The work of Ian Hacking (1975, 1990), Ulrich Beck (1992), and Anthony Giddens (1991) has laid important groundwork in this direction (see the Introduction).

3. Lotto, the most popular game in both Chania and Greece generally (according to interviews with local *lahiopraktoria* owners) is identical in almost all respects to the state lotteries of the United States; one is free to choose any six numbers between one and forty-nine—other players can also choose the same numbers—with increasingly large prizes divided between those who have matched four, five, or six of the numbers. It is played twice a week. (By contrast, in the *lahia* [lotteries] every number is picked only once from a very long series of more than a million.) The minimum cost for playing Lotto in 1995 rose from 90 Dr (a

minimum of three tries at 30 Dr each) to 150 Dr (three tries at 50 Dr each). In Lotto one has the option to play *Pro-To*. This game works more like the regular *lahia*, where each number is "owned" by only one person. By checking different boxes on one's Lotto ticket, one can choose to play only one seven-digit number or a range of such numbers, from 2 of them to 160 of them. The "base" number is always assigned by computer. As previously noted, the Greek state has introduced more games (including a second soccer pool and another lottery) since this research was conducted.

4. In the time since this research was conducted, Greece's efforts to reduce tax evasion have amplified and transformed, primarily through the application of sophisticated enforcement techniques, not surprisingly modeled on those pioneered by the United States and several countries in Europe. These new methods rely on close scrutiny of purchases (notably supported by laptop computers), both privately by business owners and in the course of business, and seek to discover discrepancies between intake and outlay. In other respects, the situation in Greece also continues to change. At the time of this writing, Greece has just participated in the largest currency transformation in modern history, as the euro was introduced as a circulating hard currency on January 1, 2002. The potential effects of the euro on tolerated criminalities such as tax evasion (and others I encountered in Chania) are the topic of my current research but cannot be included in this project.

5 Collective Solitude

> In order to play this game you must speak with the dice. If you get energy from them, it's good. If you feel a tremble from them, it's bad.
>
> —Stelios

Stelios (whose reaction to the change in Greek tax law provides the vignette that begins chapter 4), told me this as we sat at the bar of a dice gambling location in the old city. He was a dice gambler, originally from Sfakia, but he had traveled extensively and spoke some English as a result of being in the United States for twelve years. Stelios had joined a conversation I was having with the owner of the place, Mikhalis, and after a set of regular interruptions from Stelios, or perhaps because of other business down the bar, Mikhalis moved on. Stelios said that the first time that he ever gambled was when he was twelve years old, and that he lost 2 drachmas. Later, twenty-three years old in America, he went to a race track and chose a horse for a friend who bet on it despite long odds. The friend won a lot of money, and Stelios's share was US$1,200. That moment, he said, was when he knew that he was a gambler. He worked driving a cab in New York, he said, but he went to Atlantic City three times a week and to Las Vegas at least once a month. "I am a player" ("*ime pekhtis*"), he said in what was from him a familiar refrain, "not just a gambler, and a very good one."

"Did you like it there?" I asked, wondering what had brought him back to Crete. "I liked the U.S. very much," he said in English. "Do you know why? Because when I was there, especially during the eight years in prison, it was like being at the best university in the world." Though declining to reveal the reason for his incarceration, he said that there he learned "all about gambling" (*"ola ya to koumari"*). As if to underscore the veracity of his story thus far, he went on to list the prisons he knew: Sing-Sing, Ryker's Island, and one in upstate New York. "I am a professional player [*epangelmatikos pekhtis*]," he continued. "I have never worked one day in my life," although he did note his ownership of the two café-bars on the beaches west of Chania (later the focus of his consternation with regard to the tax law change). He spoke scornfully about his home region, Sfakia. His house there is that of his parents, and he hated the fact that they do not have electricity. "So you like cities?" I asked. "That's where the gambling is, isn't it?" he replied.

I asked Stelios about which games he plays, and after mentioning that dice is "his game" he said that he plays some poker, and he pulled out 14,000 Dr (about US$60) in Lotto tickets and 150,000 Dr (about US$600), a remarkable sum, in Pro-To tickets. "The jackpot is 1 billion drachmas today; I wanted to play a lot," he explained. We then moved on to talking about *zaria*, and Stelios waxed rhapsodic about the game and gambling in general. Stelios spoke about how the dice spoke to his hands. He said that you must speak with the dice (*milas me ta zaria*). "If you get energy from them," he said, "it's good. If you feel a tremble from them, it's bad." The issue, he said is whether you and the dice are "synchronized." The game was his favorite for several reasons. One is that all the money is visible, and that therefore, he said, he knows how much his opponents have and may be willing to risk. Another reason is that the game moves quickly. Also, he said that when he plays dice and other games he shows no mercy to the other players. Finally, he went on, in order to play well you must watch the details of the other players, the small things that they do differently from one roll to the next. "What does this tell you?" I asked. "You learn whether they are worried about their money, whether they are desperate. That is when you must strike." He likened his role as a good player of *zaria* to that of a sniper, lying in wait until the right moment.

Being with women is also a game and a risk, much like dice, he said. When I asked the difference, he said, "You can love a woman even after a month, but she may always leave you." *Koumari* can betray you, he continued, but it is always there and always comes back. The "high" from gambling, he said, is sustained and ends when you choose, whether you win or you lose, but with a woman it can stop of its own accord, he argued, drawing imaginary lines on the bar top to illustrate that the high goes on and on in gambling but stops with women. "So why do you play?" I asked. "That is *the* question," he replied, "and there are several reasons. First, I play because of the excitement. Second, because I know I am, and always will be, successful at it." Even when he loses he feels that the money has left him for only a little while, as an investment; he feels certain that the money is just in a "little bank" (*trapezaki*) and will always return to him. The third reason, he said, is that he does not know how long he will live, so the money does not matter.

Stelios's interview reveals many of the central issues that come to the fore in dice gambling. Equating his approach to the game with his attitude toward women and with facing his own mortality dramatically demonstrates his conviction that how he plays dice is a faithful representation of who he is as a person: confident, fearless, daring, clever, and in control of his obsession with the game (it ends when *he* chooses). However, the question of mortality reveals his own admitted lack of control over chance and suggests that this confidence has its limits; this was later confirmed by the dramatic change in persona that I witnessed a month later after the tax law change.

The embodied style that one encounters among dice gamblers, both as they play and as they talk about their playing, is perhaps the most distinctive of the many styles one encounters among players of the various games in Chania, reflecting the stated claims of many of the dice gamblers that if one believes one will win (as Stelios does even when he loses, considering the lost money as in a "little bank") then one will win. This is not quite the microconcern with one's surroundings of the poker player (articulated through the trope of *gouri*), nor is it the flashy legerdemain of the *tavli* player. Instead, to win at *zaria* calls even more than other games for "instrumental nonchalance," like that needed to carry a brimming coffee cup without spilling, a resolute confidence that is paradoxical in its firm refusal to admit of its own desire. This is the hallmark of the *pekhtis*, the player, in *zaria*.

But what in particular distinguishes dice gambling from the other forms I have examined? In contrast to poker's emphasis on reading others without being read, or backgammon's on performing one's skill and marrying it to the luck in the game in the context of others' scrutiny, *zaria* is a much simpler game, in formal terms, and because it is also much faster, it seems more than the others to place the player baldly in the illuminating spotlight of his own fortune, the question of skill formally eliminated and that of reading others greatly deemphasized. In *zaria*, even more than in backgammon, all is visible (once one is within its hidden space): Resources, results, and one's state of "grace" are revealed plainly yet with neither a particular opposing player nor a suspect mediating institution. It is this deeply personal aspect of the game that presents both a boon and a challenge to the ethnographer because the "obsession" of the players does not bring them up against performative or social indeterminacies as much as it ties closely the formal indeterminacy of the continuously tossed dice to the player's own personal struggles, involving the existential uncertainties that are so difficult for the ethnographer to apprehend (for, indeed, how can one know another?). It is for this reason that in this chapter I seek to let accounts of dice gambling events speak more for themselves, thereby to underscore the limits of social analysis in the face of such personal encounters with the indeterminate. Afterward, following promptings by the dice gamblers of Chania themselves, I turn to a consideration of Dostoevsky's *The Gambler* (1972 [1866]) to gain insight into the peculiar attitude toward chance that dice gambling exemplifies. In the end, the theme of ultimate meaning and mortality that *zaria* often provokes in gamblers' comments about the game provides the most appropriate terms for an understanding of the individually construed mode of chance engagement seen in *zaria*; I leave a fuller treatment of the issue of mortality specifically to chapter 6, where I explore the story of the life and death of one close contact and friend in Chania.

Casting One's Lot

Although the tossing of the smaller, white dice of the tavli boards seems to be everywhere in Chania, *zaria* (dice gambling; lit., "dice") is nearly invisible, and observing it therefore presented a special challenge. To enter the places where *zaria* was played proved consistently to be a difficult task, and my first hesitant and clumsy attempts at introducing the topic were met most often with a dismissive wave of the hand and advice to the effect that I should be looking in the villages for *zaria*. As one hotel handyman told me, "Those of us in the city do not play dice very often. The villagers play much more." However, in contrast to the many assertions that the highest-stakes *zaria* is more prevalent in the villages, my experience in one such village suggested that *zaria* may be more openly played outside Chania but that the stakes are significantly lower, such as in Stilos, the village where a slot machine made a brief impression on one *kafenio*'s patrons (see chapter 4). Just as often, respondents immediately asserted that dice playing is a sickness (*patholoyia*), and its players are *pathiasmeni* (a term that could be said to combine the meanings of *passionate, compulsive, obsessive*, and *afflicted*). As I began to gain entry into the secretive spaces where *zaria* takes place, I began to appreciate the strong feelings it generated among both its players and its opponents. *Zaria* is also played for much higher stakes than the other games I address here, with at times more than 100,000 Dr (about US$400) riding on a single throw of the dice. This, combined with the fact that the game's odds are 50-50 (and therefore no different statistically from flipping a coin), means that long streaks of winning and losing, with miraculous or devastating consequences, are quite common. This is the key feature of the game. Like the coin-flipping game *kefaligrammata*, *zaria* entails little in the way of concrete strategy, and reading others' intentions or performing one's own dominance apparently are of little value. But unlike the coin-flipping game played on the harbor, *zaria* is not a one-on-one game; betting relationships change frequently and often are entered into multiply. This accounts for why the contest between players is muted, despite the fact that players bet against each other. *Zaria* thus seems to share characteristics with the state lotteries and scratch ticket games in that the game consists solely in a distribution of numbers that win or lose, but unlike the state-sponsored games, in *zaria* there is no controlling institution to serve the role of opponent. The "house" would be the only potential candidate, and stories about cheating do circulate, but none of the gamblers I came to know well accused or could relate such accusations about any of the prominent locations for *zaria*. With no immediate opponent or suspect institution to fill the vacuum of opposition, in *zaria* it seems that cruel chance is indeed the only ever-present adversary.

Zaria typifies for many Chaniots the secretive and morally suspect kind of gambling indicated by the term *koumari*; the two terms, *zaria* and *koumari*, often are used interchangeably. Because the game most clearly evokes claims about addiction and sickness, as well as some of the most elaborate stories about gambling excess, one key to understanding *zaria* lies in the concept of *pathos*, a term that encompasses many sides of what is seen as the distinctive feature of dice gamblers in Chania. The difficulty in translating the concept into English is illustrated by how one Greek-English dictionary defines *pathos*: "passion, ardor, fervor, mania, obsession, emotion, feeling" (even one of its examples relates the term to gambling: "He has a passion for the races" ["*Ekhi pathos me ton ipodhromo*"]). With its multilayered meaning, Greeks use the term to frame gambling in positive and negative terms, evoking an ardent and inscrutable commitment on one hand and a dangerous addiction on the other.

In Chania, however, dice gamblers themselves used the term less often to justify the practice itself than to distinguish dice gamblers from nongamblers and from gamblers who did not play *zaria*. Stelios noted that although he played other games, *zaria* was different. "It has pathos," he said, and contrasted it with the various forms of poker, which he claimed did not involve emotion: "They're mathematical." This is an unusual comment, given how often poker was framed to me, as I noted in chapter 3, as itself distinctive, being neither a skill game nor a luck game but rather a psychological one. Of course, this characterization was most common among poker players. Although in general this pattern of claiming a distinctiveness to one's favorite game is tied to a given player's interest in claiming an association with something others cannot appreciate, the patterns that emerge in these competitive characterizations are instructive. Backgammon players implicitly and explicitly tie their skill with the game to a particular mode of social differentiation, whether national, gender-based, or otherwise, as when a better player at the "national sport" claims to be a better Greek. Poker players claim that their game entails the ability to read from others' actions and statements their true intents and resources despite proverbial claims to the contrary. *Zaria* players claim that the game, with no complexity to its odds at all, entails instead an intense emotional involvement that, combined with its very high stakes and capriciousness, renders its play the ultimate test of how one confronts the swiftly shifting currents of fortune. Again, ideas of contest against other players (Stelios's comments notwithstanding) and the application of skill recede here.

Nonetheless, *zaria* often shares with backgammon the emphasis on embodied performance because *zaria* takes place at a large table or dicing surface, surrounded by players of whom only two are actually dicing against each other at any given moment. For them or the others to enter into betting relationships entails making their amounts and chosen side known, advertising for a bet. Amid this *pazari* (market, bazaar), with many different players calling for bets and acknowledging them while simultaneously watching every bounce and roll of the dice, gaining attention for oneself can be a challenge. Some players chose not to call for bets at all and instead considered the array of offers, with a catching of the caller's eye and a short nod or quick wave of a cash-filled hand, before making a bet. However, it would be an error to consider these other players as not also performing in their own way. By forcing the callers to expose their desires and then look over the table for assenting eyes, the quiet players enjoy the advantage of keeping their interests veiled, although of course by doing so they lose the opportunity to initiate betting relationships on their own terms.

The openness of the game's results and its players' resources combined with this issue of pathos account for its devotees' insistence that the game is both more personal than others and also more clearly revelatory of one's "essential" nature. Yet *zaria* in Chania is also the most anonymous of the games I observed. Many players would not play with people they knew well, and they characterized the ties between players in the game, such as in the evening described later in this chapter, as relationships of acquaintance (*skhesis tis gnorimias*). Those around the table knew others playing or the owner slightly or through other ties, enough to learn that *zaria* was being played there on that night, but in general did not know the other players around the table. This lack of intimacy at the interpersonal level is framed by the high degree of spatial privacy, marked most clearly by the person stationed at the door or window, watching for the approach of the local police, and by such measures as heavy curtains and sliding panels. Perhaps paradoxically, it seems that within an intimate space these players engage in a common activity only with nonintimates. *Zaria* thus provokes for some of its players a rather elaborate set of embodied performance practices, while the audience is largely, and intentionally, unknown. It is not clear from watching the game that the system of the auctioning of bids alone accounts for the prevalence of dramatic personal performance. What is more, these performances do not seem, in the arena of *zaria* playing, to provoke much or any response by others, apart from perhaps helping, again, to draw attention to one's desire to bet.

As the account that begins the Introduction demonstrates, *zaria* is a game played by a group, all of whom are free to bet against each other but of whom only two players are actually rolling the dice against each other at any given time. Four dice results win (six and five and double fives, sixes, and threes), and four results lose (one and two and double ones, twos, and fours), meaning that the game has even odds (50-50).[1] With a null result (any combination other than those just mentioned; e.g., four and two) the other player of the pair then rolls, continuing in this way until a winner is determined. That winner then keeps the dice, rolling against the player to the immediate right of the loser, and so on. The game moves surprisingly quickly, pausing only every half hour (or hour, depending on the location) for payment of the house's cut (*vidhani*) by every player, often marked by an exchange of the dice for a fresh pair. The players' money is easily visible because the speed of the game necessitates quick access to one's cash. Therefore, the bills are stacked in front of the players or clutched in their hands. Only now and then, when someone has a great deal of cash on hand, are some of the resources hidden (nearby in a bag or in a different pocket), although then the player is likely to make a show of retrieving it, as did the man who asked for more from his bag behind the bar. A more detailed account of another evening's play demonstrates this atmosphere of frenetic motion and sound wherein performances are both muted and ostentatious and the rise and fall of the players' fortunes are plain to see.

Clatter and Clamor

I arrived at the bar where I had previously spoken with Stelios around midnight the night before New Year's Eve. This place had some tables and video games as well as two slot machines, but the primary attraction was in the back, hardly visible from the road through the tables, chairs, bar, and customers. A large carom-billiards pool table (i.e., lacking pockets) was the lone illuminated object in the back area, lit by a bright lamp hanging over its center. I had seen some people play billiards there previously (a rarely seen game in Crete), but only on a couple of occasions. One night when no one was playing, I asked Dhimitri, the owner, why he had bought the pool table, which he rented by the hour, and with a smile I added, "Do you have many customers who like *karom* [carom billiards]?" He laughed and played along, saying, "They play on it all the time." He then noted that when he had an opportunity to buy this table he could not pass it up. "Look! It is perfect for *zaria*. If no one plays karom on it all of the rest of the year it's worth it!"

To the left of the pool table and in front of the stairs were more video games (not working) and a television that could not be seen from the street. At this television one could gamble on horse races (all filmed ahead of time at Santa Anita Racetrack). One fed money into a box to the right of the television and used a small (and therefore easily hidden) remote control to select horses and place bets. There were two remotes, so two people could play simultaneously. The remotes could also be used to shut the television off quickly. One could place only bets to win, and the only information given on the horses were the names and odds. From time to time I saw people playing this game, but only later in the evenings.

On this particular night before New Year's Eve there was a good crowd around the carom billiard table in the back. By the door in front a young man sat and watched for police. Stelios was playing, as were about eleven others when I arrived. This number varied as the evening went on, the general trend being that fewer and fewer played into the late hours. Dhimitri told me that everyone had started playing around 8 P.M. Several of the players had low stools, which they sat on around the table, mostly along the back wall. I recognized Stelios as he sat in the middle of the left side of the table, sometimes standing, as did many of the others with seats.

The players kept their money either in their hands or neatly piled on the table edge in front of them. However, because this edge was also where bets were placed, most of the players kept their money in hand; placing the money on the edge did not seem to risk confusing it with money that was bet, but many of the players who held their money pulled bills from their hand in a deliberate manner, to count them to themselves or to other players with whom they had established a betting relationship, afterwards placing the money on the table edge. Most of the players had at least a good amount of 1,000- and 5,000-Dr bills, with an average of about 50,000 Dr (about US$200) showing.

Play proceeded around the table with two players at any given time dicing against each other, the dice shifting between them when the result of a throw was inconclusive (*tipota*). Once one of them won, he then diced against the next person in the circle (counterclockwise), and so on. Thus, at any given time, the distance between the two dicing players in the circle was an index of how long the previous winner (the one to the left of the other player) has been winning, being at least as long as the distance between them in players. I asked players about this and about how they decided on whom to bet. The answers varied widely, as one might expect, but several said that it did make a difference how long someone had been winning, meaning that they were less likely to bet for him generally. "However," one contact said, "if he has been winning all night, then why not bet on him? You can lose this time but win [over the course of] the whole evening."

How do the patterns not only of winning and losing but also of the bets themselves emerge and get acted upon over the course of an evening? There is a regular rhythm, alternating between the throws of the dice and the betting or paying in between wins, and I began to get a sense of the flow of the money as well, over time becoming aware of who had been recently losing money or had been gaining it, with the corresponding expansion and contraction of the stacks and wads of money semi-regularly spaced around the table. On this particular night, I noted one of many consistent betting relationships, the course of which constituted a subplot to the game. Stelios had told me a few days earlier, "Sometimes, not every time, one sees that one has an enemy at the table, someone who bets against you continually, [or] even more someone who has in his eyes a look that says he is your enemy."

Bets took place between any two players who wished, many players at times taking on multiple betting opponents, others sitting out at any given time. The negotiation of bets is the most complicated aspect of the entire process. A player who would like to bet with someone calls out "*egho*" or "*esi*" to indicate whether he would like to bet for the current shooter or against him (for the other shooter). Often this player called out "*egho*" or "*esi*" and an amount of money, usually at the same time putting the money down in front of him. As he continued to try to find a bet, he might become a bit of a salesman, pointing to the money and gesturing or calling out other phrases. If another player wanted to take such a bet, he could make eye contact with the caller, gesture, or say something to affirm the bet (often "*pai*" or "*pane*," "it's going" or "they're going"). Also, every half-hour, the bar collected its share. A burly man brought a new set of dice to the table (they alternated between a clear green set and a clear red set), and each player paid 1,000 Dr.

Because of the large size of the billiard table (much larger than those described in the opening example, which were tables custom-made for *zaria*), some cooperation was called for, manifested in several ways. First, because the players at one end often could not see the dice result if they stopped at the other end, a player near the dice called out the result if it won or lost, or "*tipota*" if it did neither. This was not always the case, and sometimes one had to ask for the result. Also, to send the dice back down the table to the shooter, a player near a die rolled it back down the table. Again, this was not always the case, and a player often rolled back only a die right next to him, ignoring the one only a few inches away. The table also called for cooperation in managing the winnings. If a player won a bet from a player a good distance away, that player tried to throw or toss the money down the table, but it often did not make it all the way, in which case someone in between had to move it along, often after several requests by the player waiting for it. Finally, players also shared cigarettes. One asked, often it seemed from across the table, for a cigarette, and the smoker threw a pack to him, who after taking one threw it back, both tosses often happening with a bit of a snap or spin.

Stelios said that every gambler has his or her own style. He likes to get in and get out quickly, to take the other players' money rapidly. He compared other gamblers' style of taking one's time to being like a sniper, waiting and waiting. Between certain players, particularly between Stelios and the player in the front middle of the table, who bet against each other frequently all evening, there was a quality not so much of competition as of mutual enjoyment in the whole game. At least one reason why these qualities are possible is that over time at the table players begin to know each other's betting patterns, to the extent that they have them. Some gamblers tended, at least for a period of time, to bet regularly for one player or another, for example. Thus, Stelios looked at this other player as he called for a bet and perhaps even said, questioningly,

"*Pane?*" and then, as the other player took the bet, he might say, "*Pane*" (perhaps after the other player had said it) and smiled with excitement. This is in marked contrast to nearly every other game I describe in this work, where the antagonistic quality of the relationship between opponents is ever-present. It is also at odds with Stelios's own interpretation of his relationship with other bettors at the *zaria* table, seen in his comments at the start of this chapter. I surmise that Stelios's love of an audience may have contributed to his overdramatization of the situation when he first presented it to me.

Players used many methods to call for bets. In particular, if the player who currently had the dice wanted bets, he dropped the dice a short distance onto the table directly in front of him with a pattering sound, then pulled his hand away from them slightly. At the same time, he looked around the room and again called for bets. As with other parts of the practice, some players had more distinct styles in this respect than others. For example, Stelios dropped the dice and spread wide both his arms, sometimes saying, "Come, now, someone must want to bet." Certainly the most visible aspect of personal style was how a given player chose to throw the dice. One player shook the dice until he stopped his hands on the upswing, the dice making a clearly audible click at that moment, after which he threw them across the table. Other players "lofted" the dice rather than throwing them more laterally; at one point the dice hit one of the lamps above the pool table during such an attempt. Like a few others, Stelios shook the dice very close to his ear, and appeared to be listening to them, a gesture that recalled his remarks to me about conversing with the dice.

Also related to the issue of style is the money itself and the degree to which players were aware of how much they lost or won. In certain ways—particularly in how a player called for a bet on his entire stack and only counted it afterward, and then only if the bet was won—the players in general appeared not to be too concerned about the amounts of money they were betting. *Appeared* is important here because this is just one of the different indications of awareness of loss or gain. In other ways, such as a player's violent and contemptuous throw of larger amounts of money across the table when they were lost, it was clear that players knew how much they lost. There is a noticeable difference in such cases with regard to the bettor's demeanor before and after the result. A player may bet a stack of bills without counting it, and then, his lack of concern for the amount established, count it out very carefully when the loser is to pay him. Thus, the ethos of imprecision, where among those with whom one has established a degree of intimacy there is little overt concern with monetary exactitude (see Herzfeld 1991, 168), has its limits here, particularly as one has an opportunity to evince both attitudes without fear of noticeable contradiction. The important point is that the conditions of indeterminacy in *zaria* are active while the bet is placed, so nonchalance in the face of this unpredictability is appropriate at that time. After the bet, although an unconcerned demeanor still has value with reference to money, the indeterminate moment has faded, and the bettor can get on with receiving the appropriate—that is, precise—amount of money.

The display of money in the way typical of *zaria* playing is not unique to the game. Many Chaniot men whom I knew carried their cash in a folded (once) or rolled wad in a front pocket of their jeans or trousers. I was often struck by the size of the clutch of bills they often thus removed, invariably and deliberately peeling off the appropriate amount. The denominations of the bills almost always appeared large as well (5,000- and 10,000-Dr), implying that the wad as a whole amounted to hundreds of thousands of drachmas (possibly thousands of dollars). But this poetics of monetary display has its own forms of deception, of course, because 1,000-Dr bills (each worth about US$4), were close enough in size to the larger bills to pass for them, en masse, as long as a few large denominations were wrapped around the bundle. To be sure, in *zaria* situations this was less possible because the stack was constantly on display and, to allow quick access, was rarely folded or wrapped.

An Essential Reference

In *zaria*, then, very little stands between the player and the continuously and quickly unfolding outcomes that signal ruination or redemption. The results of the dice are in plain view, as is the player's money, for the most part. The question of skill is muted by the straightforwardness of the game, and the speed with which it moves contributes to the player's or spectator's ability to follow the rise and fall of a given player's fortune. The stance toward indeterminacy that characterizes *zaria*, then, is that of "instrumental nonchalance," because in the face of these rapid and fickle judgments the only tenable solution is to be a rock amid the storm. Conversations with many of the dice gamblers bore this out, and this was understandably a source of pride on their part. "*Zaria* is the true test," one such player told me.

But reference to this disposition, though common enough among many of the *zaria* players with whom I spoke, nonetheless is not sufficient to account for how many of them appeared to me: staring bleakly at the dice, their eyes alone following their path across the table, then paying off or collecting until the next result. As they struggled, it seemed, in the gambling arena that reveals most starkly their own positions amid the tides of chance, the mixture of frustration, fascination, and bewilderment they evinced brought to my mind how Stelios had looked and talked that day, worried about the new tax laws and faced with the real possibility of losing his businesses. Their predicament provides a cautionary tale here as it brings to light a vulnerability at most times hidden in Chania, both in the games I have described and in everyday experience. It also attests to the limits of ethnographic inquiry because standard techniques of interviewing and observation did little to illuminate the existential disposition I saw in action among them.

In such a context, where the deeply personal aspects of the gambling experience seem to take precedence over or even to exclude any social or institutional ones, a turn to the work of Dostoevsky, one of the great writers of what Thomas Mann called "psychological lyricism" (Mann 1945, ix), may provide some illumination. This is ethnographically appropriate because several of the gamblers themselves mentioned Dostoevsky's *The Gambler,* claiming that he had captured the essence (*ousia*) of the gambler's experience. One gambler went so far as to refuse to discuss the issue of gambling further until I had read the work.

The last of Dostoevsky's short novels, *The Gambler* was published on the heels of some of Dostoevsky's greatest works, immediately after *Crime and Punishment.* Dictated under financial pressure to a stenographer over the course of roughly three weeks, it was written at a time when Dostoevsky himself was struggling with obsessive gambling, and it may be the most autobiographical of Dostoevsky's works (Mann 1945; Wasiolek 1972; Coulson 1966). As Wasiolek (1972, xxxi) writes, "The recklessness with which [Dostoevsky] divested himself of whatever money he made suggests that he enjoyed being without money more than having it. He expressed frequently a contempt for money, especially for money accumulated in any systematic way, a practice he identified especially with the German mentality. At the roulette table, no matter how large the temporary winnings, he would play until he lost everything he had. He seemed at peace with himself only when there was nothing left and no possibility of gaining more."

Wasiolek further suggests that Dostoevsky wrote *The Gambler* as part of an attempt to come to terms with his own obsessive pursuit of gambling. A full account of even a short novel by an author of such depth is impossible here, but, briefly put, it tells the story of Aleksei Ivanovich, a young man obsessed, at the start of the tale, with both a young woman and with gambling, and in the end it is clear that he sees roulette as his only salvation. A twenty-five-year-old university graduate and a member of the nobility, he is without money and is therefore forced to accompany a general and his family as a teacher. He endures a complex relationship of mutual love and hate with the general's stepdaughter, Polina (modeled after a young writer whom Dostoevsky pursued shortly before writing *The Gambler*). He hopelessly loves her and would do anything for her, yet he also hates her and could sometimes, he states, kill her. His game is roulette (which my contacts noted was a similar game to *zaria* given the clear and stark odds and the blatant pitting of man against chance), and shortly after being dismissed because of an embarrassing scene he creates at the instigation of Polina, he quite unusually wins a small fortune at the tables. He presents the money to Polina, and she spends the night with him but then throws the money in his face and leaves, joining the honest, laconic Englishman, Astley. Aleksei retaliates by going to Paris with Blanche, a professional courtesan who had pursued the general, because in exchange for money she promises Aleksei a month of riotous living. Blanche spends all the money, calls Aleksei a fool, and finally leaves him to marry the general after all. His life then becomes an endless round of roulette, debts, and poverty. Astley locates him and reports that Polina loves him but forecasts that he will be ruined and spend the rest of his life at roulette. He decides to prove to her that he is a man, but his actions are limited to musing about how he could change his fate by winning at roulette.[2]

As in much of Dostoevsky's work, the main characters, Aleksei and Polina, are passionate as well as criminal—criminal in the sense that they do not give much weight to following the strictures of either social convention or formal law. This alone may account for the attractiveness of the story for some Chaniots as a portrait of the *zaria* gambler point of view, particularly given the close relationships between criminality, passion, and gambling in Chania that I have noted in this chapter and elsewhere. Yet there is more to the tale, I suggest, that can help us understand its particularly potent applicability for the highly personal and even isolated context of dice gambling. One of the more evident features of Aleksei's position that is shared by that of many of the Chaniot dice gamblers (at least as they presented it to others) is a combination of social marginalization and freedom, a freedom that can allow for the resistance of social hierarchies, a phenomenon familiar to anthropologists in the concept of the liminal state. Wasiolek (1972, xxxiii) describes this quality of Aleksei's position as follows: "Aleksei is a person without social consequences, disdained by all; yet he comes to terrify those who disdain him and to dominate those who are his social superiors. He is a buffoon, a social maladroit, a lackey, but he chooses his roles and as such is superior to them. He . . . knows that multiple identities and denials give him an advantage over those who define, fix, and cling to their identities." One could hardly better characterize the ideology of resistance to central authority that characterizes what Cretans self-consciously call "the Cretan mentality." It is a self-confidence borne of self-reliance and of freely chosen roles, even though (and perhaps because) they fall outside the conventional. As Wasiolek also notes, indeterminate situations provide just the kind of opportunity for this kind of identity construction.

But the essence of the gambler that Dostoevksy captured, according to my contacts, was not this quality so much as the pathos for gambling itself, a passion that overruns all other spheres of life, that is thus situated between the concepts of obsession, sickness, addiction, and passion. Dostoevsky's work was a means for them to convey to me the concept of pathos, something they felt they could not translate or otherwise convey on their own, in Greek or English. Reference to a work of literature becomes the only way to convey an experience that escapes conventional forms of communication. Aleksei begins the story attempting to balance his obsessions with Polina and roulette, spending equal amounts of thought (we hear the tale from his point of view) scheming to obtain her and scheming to obtain money for the tables. By the end of the story, however, all concerns other than gambling have been rendered away from him, and this totalizing quality of chance in his life is, I think, very close to what the Chaniot gamblers were trying to express to me. Wasiolek again characterizes this aspect of Aleksei's life helpfully:

> Before the climactic scene . . . he had pursued love and power over others. . . . He was alive with plans, goals, and the feelings of accomplishment. Now he seems like a man drained of the goals and motives that had driven him. We can now conclude merely that what had driven him before, he now recognizes as illusion. Love, social importance, and even money hold no importance for him. . . .
> The daring to risk the last gulden on the irrational turn of the wheel gives him what the fixities of position, money, and love do not; the feeling of being open to the irrationalities of the turning wheel, and one suspects for Dostoevsky, the irrationalities of human life. (Wasiolek 1972, xxxvi)

Like the Chaniot gamblers who watched the tumbling of dice with staring, bloodshot eyes, Aleksei does not pursue this kind of stark gambling simply for monetary profit or as part of complex performative pursuits of local social standing. He does not even pursue it merely to resist domination by national or institutional structures and strictures. In the end, he, and they, pursue this kind of gambling because to engage chance baldly, in this manner, is part of a way to constitute their selves. In an arena where most of the intricate webs of Chaniot social relations are intentionally stripped away, and where not even the state intercedes, these players are left alone, among many, to face the rise and fall of their fortunes.

Although I have had to venture into a more speculative mode in this chapter to confront analytically a game in which the experience and engagement of indeterminacy is so primary, I consider this reading consistent with the places in this work where the stance of instrumental nonchalance arises. To illustrate this disposition more thoroughly, however, I turn in chapter 6 to the case of a close friend and contact who died shortly after I left Chania. Just as Stelios linked his pathos for *zaria* to his confrontation with his own mortality, Nikos presented his own stance toward the indeterminate through a set of his experiences leading up to his death. I am sure that it will not go unremarked that gambling plays almost no role in the portrait I try to paint of him. This is intentional: By applying the ideas about indeterminacy developed throughout this work to a situation in which the stakes are perhaps highest of all, that of mortality, I hope to show how important it is to improve our approach to indeterminacy as it occurs throughout human experience.

Notes

1. To be precise, five outcomes win and five lose because the nondouble results can happen two ways (i.e., five-six or six-five and one-two or two-one). Thus, of the thirty-six possible outcomes from two dice, five win, five lose, and twenty-six are null results.

2. For this plot summary I am indebted to the concise account in Richard Chapple's *A Dostoevsky Dictionary* (1983, 152–59).

6 Confronting Consequences

"Tora!" ("Now!") exclaimed my friend Nikos as the coffee began to froth and bubble, threatening to overflow the long-handled brass coffeepot. I stirred the coffee briskly as I removed it from the flame, trying to do everything just as I had seen Nikos do it many times. My next problem: the flame. It was produced by a small propane canister with a burner attached to the top; the heat from it struck my face as soon as I moved the pot away. Somehow Nikos always turned off the burner while simultaneously stirring the pot he held. How had he done this? All of this flashed through my mind as I finally began to look for a spot to set the spoon down before reaching under the flame to turn off the burner. But it was already off; Nikos had reached around behind me and deftly extinguished it. Now the next part of the lesson: pouring the coffee into a small cup, ideally without splashing any coffee on the saucer. *"Ohi etsi—apo psila"* ("Not that way—from up high"), Nikos chided. The coffee poured to the brim—not without some errant splashes—and, gripping the saucer's edge in the fingers of my right hand, I began to carry it to our table. The cup trembled and rattled as I moved across the floor, the more so, it seemed, the more I watched it intently, and coffee began to overflow, staining the white exterior of the cup and running down to the saucer. "Here," said Nikos as he took the cup and saucer away from me. And then, pointing forward by cutting the air in front of his face sharply with the edge of a vertically raised hand, he said, "You must look forward. Only. The cup is nothing. Nothing! Only then will it not spill."

And so went a brief lesson in the midst of a quiet afternoon on the island of Crete.[1] Nikos, along with his two brothers, owned a small hotel in the old town, where we spent many such afternoons. I came to understand much better later, after his death, just what Nikos was teaching me that afternoon as the coffee cup shimmied in my hand. He was putting forward an approach to the contingent, a way to face the unpredictable, whether it be the possibility of spillage or something more serious, such as the timing of his impending liver failure. I do not mean to imply that this approach was a fully verbalized, coherent, and systematic way of confronting the unexpected (nor do I suggest that this particular account does not demonstrate a technique well known to anyone who has waited tables for a living), but through this example and others from his life, I piece together a portrait of how Nikos engaged the uncertainties of his life. These examples demonstrate that this approach was more a technique, a learned disposition toward the world that revealed itself in actions and in reflections. It is encapsulated in the paradoxical injunction to ignore my concern (the coffee) in order to attain my goal (not spilling it), and it is a personal engagement of chance that I will try to make sense of throughout much of this chapter. Nikos once said to me that the biggest risk in the world was friendship; opening oneself up to another, he said, was what made one most vulnerable. For him, risk and uncertainty were inextricably bound up in social relations and personal comportment, and this suggests that any view that begins from the assumption that risk is dangerous (and should be minimized or avoided) must be questioned. Instead, his views indicate that it is through the performative engagement of chance, rather than through its minimization or resolution (such as through statistical "risk management"), that one may demonstrate socially one's place vis-à-vis chance and, by extension, one's place in relation to others and the world.

Nikos died on a moped while heading home one evening in 1996 when, apparently, he fainted from liver failure and crashed into the back of a parked truck. I write *apparently* advisedly because, as this chapter explores, there were multiple accountings for his death, and no one of them can claim precedence. In the end, his final moments were his alone. It was an event that happened after I had left the field and of which I was informed nearly immediately by mutual friends and Nikos's family. My coming to terms with this event involved attempting to reconcile this chanceful event into some meaningful account, a process that mirrors how social actors in general engage the unpredictable. I seek to use this parallel constructively here to move beyond the context of gambling specifically and explore how the insights developed here may help us understand the role of contingency in social life even in such tragic circumstances. In particular, I explore the disjuncture between one person's disposition toward death and the various attempts by others to account for an unforeseen, in this case horrible event.

I have argued throughout this work that conventional approaches to understanding contingency in experience are in deep need of fundamental reappraisal, and in particular I assert that they preclude a clear understanding of engagements of chance both at the personal level (where an attitude toward chance, such as Nikos's, is nonetheless embedded in local understandings of chance) and at the level of local struggles over accountability (where the legitimacy of institutions may rest on their ability to account for an unforeseen event according to a particular way of accounting for chance). Instead, I have argued for a model for examining contingency that avoids normative assumptions, helps us begin to sort out the various kinds and sources of indeterminacy, and provides a groundwork for assessing the struggles over accountability that characterize a surprisingly large part of everyday life.

I present a part of Nikos's life here as a final illustration of the engagements of chance across its sources that I discuss throughout this work. I seek to give a sense of his personal attitude toward chance, one that is lost in applying the traditional academic discourse of risk. I finally briefly consider Nikos's death and the attempts by various locals to "explain" it, attempts that reveal how accounting for the contingent is a process, embedded in local and national struggles over meaning and resources, which occupies a central and contested position in social life: Contingency mediates and shapes the struggles over resources and identity that characterize everyday life from the local to the national level.

The Eagle Dies in Midflight

I met Nikos in one of the chance meetings so common to fieldwork: I paused outside the hotel he owned with his brothers to examine the picture of a room they had posted by the door. Within a few moments Nikos had engaged me in conversation and invited me inside their small café. He began to ply me with multiple toasts of *raki* (a strong, locally made, unaged brandy) while we spoke about everything from backgammon to the status of the old town of Chania. I came to realize that to describe this meeting as "by chance" is itself incomplete because Nikos was quite adept at engaging passersby, particularly foreigners, both to get to know them and, of course, to get them to stay at his hotel. Furthermore, Nikos worked the afternoon shift at the hotel (from 2 until 8 P.M., his brothers taking the other two shifts), a time when many shops close for a brief siesta and during which it is mostly tourists and other foreigners out and about.

Nikos was in his early forties and was the oldest of the three brothers. He had a thin build and a rakish smile and dressed almost exclusively in black. One of the first things I learned from him was that a cousin of his who lived in the United States and owned a fast-food hamburger place in Virginia had recently been shot and killed in a robbery attempt, and it was for this reason, Nikos said, that he wore black. Yet he continued to wear this color throughout the two years that I knew him, and he later said that he favored darker colors because they "suited his character." Nikos's family was originally from a high mountain village southeast of Chania, located in the Sfakia region of the island. Nikos's father had long run a very successful *kafenio* in their neighborhood in Chania. He passed along the money he had saved to his sons, who bought a property in the old town. The hotel they built on the site was a success, and they also rented a space on its first floor to a small restaurant that also enjoyed good business. At the time I met him, Nikos was pleased to be able to provide for his own family (a wife and two daughters), yet his comments about his children, particularly about their future, were always tinged by an element of sadness. It was only after I came to know him better that I realized that it was his failing health that led him to expect not to see his daughters grow into adulthood.

Nikos confronted the uncertainty that lies at the root of much of social life, that of his own mortality, through a degenerative liver condition, the result of years of constant drinking. Although his death was inevitable, it was, as for almost everyone, the timing that could not be predicted. As Weber observed (1946, 335), "Since death is a fate that comes to everyone, nobody can ever say why it comes precisely to him and why it comes just when it does." How much of his daughters' childhood would Nikos be able to see? In thinking about mortality and risk, one might be tempted to see death as the most unambiguously undesirable of events, the arrival of which should be fought continually. Yet we must consider the possibility revealed in a quote by an Inuit woman in a piece on perceptions of risk by Patricia Kaufert and John O'Neil (1993, 49): "Can you guarantee my life tomorrow? . . . There's always risk. I mean, you wouldn't live if you didn't live with risks." This quote suggests that even impending death may be the occasion for the constitution of selfhood; that is, facing this contingency may be an essential part of living and may therefore reflect how one faces, rather than avoids or minimizes, contingency elsewhere in life. Nikos's approach to these circumstances thus mirrored his approach to uncertainties generally, I suggest, and could be characterized as a particular manifestation of instrumental nonchalance, an approach that, like carrying a brimming cup, relied on a resolute insistence that the outcome was, paradoxically, simultaneously unimportant yet central. One sees here a claim on his part about facing mortality that relies on the bringing together of the performative domain of indeterminacy (carrying the cup) with the formal (death's timing) and cosmologic domains (its meaning). (Later in this chapter I explore an example wherein Nikos also brought the social domain of indeterminacy into play.)

Nikos took minimal steps to alleviate his condition, did not follow his doctor's recommendations, and continued to present himself as unconcerned about what might befall him. This is precisely the approach to contingency that Campbell (1964) cautioned strongly against reading as fatalism. To do so would be to miss the centrality of the engagement of chance that this example presents and that characterizes a heretofore underrecognized element of human experience everywhere. Indeed, charges of fatalism are the inevitable result when an attitude toward chance that does not accord with a risk management approach finds public expression. But rather than a bowing down to destiny, Nikos's instrumental nonchalance was the ultimate act against it, stating, as Nikos did to me, that he would not let an impending doom change who he was.[2] This statement strikes at the heart of social analysts' own preconceptions about the normative undesirability of contingency.

Although space does not permit me to give a full account of Nikos's life, I hope that the pieces I describe here combined with the anecdote that begins this chapter paint a full enough picture of him, in particular that they reveal something of the way in which he engaged chance in his life. I do not intend to give the impression that Nikos had a single, coherent, formalized paradigm for making sense of the indeterminate in his life; in fact, I am wary of any approach that oversystematizes action. Instead, I seek to portray both Nikos's actions and his reflections to convey a portrait of how, in myriad domains of experience, often through embodied techniques such as in the example of the coffee cup, he faced his illness and mortality. I seek to create a portrait that is more nuanced than that which a surface reading of his actions might suggest, one that probably would be labeled as fatalistic and thereby irrational.

The most obvious example of how Nikos rejected certain approaches to chance that might be called statistical is provided by a contrast he drew between his style of playing backgammon and that of his brother. Bobbis played slowly, he said, always taking time to check all the possibilities. Indeed, this difference in tempo was something I had noticed in Bobbis's backgammon playing, along with the fact that the two did not often play together. Nikos played the game with a lively, though not at all frenetic, pace, one that I came to adopt and enjoy from our frequent games together. Nikos remarked (and later demonstrated, with the backgammon board) that in certain situations most players will stop the game, one of them conceding that the game is essentially over (usually with a double loss). Nikos took the board and laid out such a situation. He pointed out that an extremely unlikely streak of double twos (six in a row, a chance of roughly one in 2 billion) for the player playing the black would mean that the white player has a chance of winning. Bobbis, he said, would *always* play these situations out, on the minuscule chance that he might win.

For most of these situations, Nikos said, "Not even those in prison would play that out!" (*"Dhen to paizoune oute i filakismeni!"*), making forcefully the point that even if one had nothing else to do with one's time it would not be worthwhile to finish such a game.[3] Nikos's accusation of unreasonableness on the part of Bobbis is particularly noteworthy here because it is Bobbis's strict reliance on a statistical possibility, so often equated with rationality in academic literature, that renders his conduct, in Nikos's eyes, impossible to comprehend, even irrational. I asked Nikos why he does not play this way, and he said that he just does not like to do so. His brother plays well, Nikos emphasized, "but I do not like to play that way." "Why?" I pressed. "For me," he said, "to play quickly, and to have the other player play quickly, creates *parea*" (a sense of good company). "The experience is better?" I asked. "Yes," he answered, "It's better for the *kefi* [sociable enjoyment] of the game." So Nikos extends his criticism of his brother to social terms, where reliance on statistics for one's decisions about the play of the game runs counter to sociability and a good feeling or atmosphere (*kefi*). Therefore, for Nikos the ensuing game is as much about creating a common intimate space through a common approach to the game as it is about a contest between two individuals.

To return, then, to Nikos's comments on friendship as the greatest risk one can face, I am reminded of an evening, late in my fieldwork, when, according to the Orthodox calendar, it was my nameday (the Sunday one week after Orthodox Easter). At that time I was staying with another Chaniot friend and contact, Alekos, a ceramicist who was distinguished from most other Chaniots by his utter lack of interest in gambling and the more illicit aspects of Chaniot life that I was examining at the time. The contrast between him and Nikos (from whom I had learned most of the gambling games played in Chania and met many useful contacts) was considerable. To mark my nameday Alekos had planned a very simple yet delicious dinner on the front patio of his house above Chania. Most Greeks would expect on their nameday to receive friends at their business or home all day long and be ready to provide them with sweets or drinks. Because I had no recognizable and known residence in the city at that time (I had left a place there where I had stayed all year shortly before) or a place of business where friends could find me, I had instead spent the day walking from one friend's place to another with a box of pastries for each one. At the end of the afternoon, Nikos asked where I was going. "Home," I replied simply, expecting then to say goodbye and be on my way. "I'll drive you," Nikos said, an unusual offer from him, and before I knew it we were, at my direction, heading up the hill east of the city to the high plateau known as Akrotiri, where Alekos lived.

Nikos stopped at a bakery and bought some cookies and then went next door to buy some Greek brandy. "What are you doing?" I asked him. "One does not visit someone's house empty-handed," Nikos replied, looking at me as if wondering how I could have forgotten a custom I knew as well as my own name. His evasive reply made me all the more nervous. Alekos was not the sort to have socialized with Nikos and, in our conversations about my work, had long expressed puzzlement about why I might want to spend so much time with these, in his words, unpredictable scoundrels. When he then heard that Nikos was from Sfakia originally, his wariness increased. Therefore, as I was heading toward Alekos's house with someone he neither expected nor was likely to want to entertain, my apprehension grew. In this situation the presence of social indeterminacy was so intense as to be palpable. Yet Nikos charged forward. What prompts such an unexpected and, in terms of its outcome, unpredictable action? I can only point out that this engagement of indeterminacy, here of the social kind, reflected again Nikos's engagement of it elsewhere. It is also worthwhile to note that this attention to the contingent context and quality of social action also helps us to avoid seeing social performance as the rote execution of conventional social practices. As theorists of performance have long recognized (Bauman 1977; Herzfeld 1985), it is the innovative application and combination of convention that creates new social forms and reflects true social virtuosity; as the evening continued, Nikos continued to demonstrate this fearless facility.

When we arrived, Alekos gave us a strained but polite smile as Nikos produced the pastries and brandy and presented them to Alekos. Alekos then asked, somewhat forcedly, whether Nikos would stay for dinner, whereupon Nikos replied, "Of course! It is Thomas's nameday, didn't you expect company?" The evening continued, with much wine and food, and included Nikos's delighted discovery of a radio station playing *zeibekiko* music, distinguished by the solo male dance that accompanies it, the performance of which is often put forth as the hallmark of manhood and Greekness (see Cowan 1990). Of course, it was not long before Nikos was entreating me to give the difficult improvisational dance a try, and as I was dancing (and presumably getting it at least a little right), I suddenly heard the crash of dishware as Nikos hurled a small plate near my feet. Alekos's reaction was immediate; he grabbed the more precious items of dishware from the table (those that he had made himself) and retreated a bit from the area. Nikos forcefully glossed over any discomfort, just as he had when he arrived. *"Bravo, Thoma* [Thomas]!" he cried, and engaged Alekos in agreeing with him that I had indeed learned at least a little during my time on Crete. By the end of the evening even Alekos had come to enjoy himself, standing up for a dance as well. This story demonstrates Nikos's approach to social relations, even those that might be fraught with the unexpected. Knowing that I would have evaded any direct attempt to have him join me with Alekos, he proceeded directly and forcefully, as if holding a brimming cup, one could say, full of either my anxiety or the possible social consequences. He charged forward and, in the end, instigated an evening I will never forget. It was as the three of us chatted, late into the night, that Nikos first told me that the greatest risk in life was friendship, and I only later appreciated how that evening was its perfect demonstration.

Shortly before I left Chania Nikos and I went out one evening to a dance club owned by a friend of his. It was a crowded, popular place for Chaniots in the middle of the city, and its clientele was varied in age, from those in their early twenties to early fifties. The music was a mixture of Greek popular music and international dance music (much of it from the United States), and it was not long before a song came on that Nikos proclaimed his favorite. He interrupted my conversation with another friend and told me to listen to the words carefully. It was a song by a Greek pop music group, titled *"O aetos petheni ston aera"* ("The Eagle Dies in Mid-Flight" [lit., in the air]). He then proceeded to dance a *zeibekiko* to the song, a highly unusual action that initially brought critical stares from those around us. Nikos danced skillfully, however, and it was not long before those around us were watching intently and applauding at the artful near-stumbles that the dance requires and that Nikos performed beautifully. *Zeibekiko* calls for a convincing presentation of oneself as always on the brink of disaster (about to fall) yet at the last minute able to snatch success (regaining balance) out of the jaws of capricious fate. Through success in this performative domain of indeterminacy (indeed, one that foregrounds the indeterminacy to a remarkable degree), I suggest that Nikos was able both to comment upon and to constitute his own approach toward his mortality. I thought about the song's lyrics as I watched him. Although I did not bring up the subject to him explicitly, to me the idea of facing one's mortality while being true to who one is—what the song's title suggested—combined with the dance's similar injunction to dance on the brink of failure, together elegantly portrayed how Nikos engaged his impending mortality. It also showed that to have done otherwise (by attempting to reduce his risk by complying with doctor's recommendations, for example) would have compromised his sense of self.

———————

Nikos's death was a puzzle for me and his friends and family. In my later visits to Chania I joined his daughters, wife, and mother in remembering him, and I talked to others who knew him. Just as Nikos's personal attitude toward chance illustrates how engagements of the contingent may be constitutive of self, a possibility that approaches based on risk miss, I contend that an examination of these other accounts of his death can begin to open our eyes to a broader case: the politics of contingency, an arena where the legitimacy of institutions, groups, and individuals is at stake.

It is notable that although traffic accidents as an issue have appeared only sporadically in anthropological literature (Moore 1987; Frankenberg 1993), in each of these cases the authors have presented them as particularly useful "diagnostic events" (in Moore's terms). As Moore (1987, 730) writes, "The kind of event that should be privileged is one that reveals ongoing contests and conflicts and competitions and the efforts to prevent, suppress, or repress these." Traffic accidents can pose a challenge for both official and unofficial perspectives. At the official level (and by this I do not mean simply that of the nation-state but any formal vehicle for disseminating information, such as newspapers and other media outlets), they suggest the failure of institutional systems of authority to ensure continuity, and they therefore demand a coherent response. Again, as Weber noted, this is perhaps more the result of these institutions seeking to guarantee their legitimacy over time than a result of the desires of the individuals they seek to protect. At the unofficial level, and despite the accountings put forth officially, such events can raise questions of responsibility that can never be fully resolved.

My primary goal throughout this work has been to demonstrate how much is lost in conventional approaches to understanding contingency, and Nikos's story shows this particularly well on the level of personal attitudes toward chance. However, Nikos's death was a small one in the broader context of the ongoing events that occupy the residents of Chania on a day-to-day basis, and it certainly did not touch the broader level of national discourse, such as that represented by the Greek national daily newspapers. It was nonetheless front-page news locally in Chania the day after it happened. On that day, the largest local newspaper, *Chaniotika Nea*, ran a small story on the front page with the headline, "41-Year Old Killed on the Road [lit., in traffic]." It included a small picture of Nikos (from his official Greek identity card) with the caption "The unfortunate [*atikhos*] Nikos B." and a larger picture of a moped with the caption "A motorcycle such as this led to the tragic death of a 41-year-old Chaniot." The story itself recounts the circumstances of Nikos's death from a particular point of view. He died when the moped he was driving collided with a parked truck, the article says, and it notes that the moped and the truck had the appropriate licenses. The picture of the moped dominates the article, and its prominence is consistent with the newspaper's regular articles and editorials on traffic problems and dangers in Chania and Crete more generally. There was no follow-up article to mention that Nikos collided with the truck when he lost control of his moped because his liver failed, as an autopsy soon revealed, rather than as a result of, for example, poor traffic conditions. (His family at first suspected that he had been drinking that evening and had lost control of the moped while drunk, but the autopsy revealed that he had a minimal amount of alcohol in his system.) The discourse of traffic safety in Greece often focuses on the profusion of mopeds and motorcycles on the roads, and in particular the lack of, or lack of enforcement of, laws requiring helmets. Motorcycle accidents in particular are an ever-present issue in the country, and very few people do not have a relative who was at least seriously injured while riding a motorcycle or moped. For *Chaniotika Nea*, Nikos's death was an opportunity to present yet another example of the dangers of *papaki* (moped) use, underscored by the placing of a large photograph of a similar moped in the middle of the article's text, with only Nikos's smaller Greek identity card photograph off to one side. The issue in this account, then, was not Nikos's personal qualities as a moped operator or even as someone who might have been drinking. The idea that an error in performance on his part might have been the root cause of his death is not present. Instead, the contingencies of the traffic system itself (with its congestion, its attendant laws, and their lack of enforcement), an indeterminacy that we might describe as belonging to the formal domain, is the thrust of the coverage. A case such as Nikos's thus becomes fuel to a fire of criticism of government management of traffic conditions.

The accounts of Nikos's death from other sources differed widely from that of *Chaniotika Nea*. A friend of Nikos, a jewelry store owner, mentioned that Nikos was "born into the wrong era" (*"yenithike lathos epokhi"*), a sentiment echoed by a few of his other acquaintances. "What do you mean?" I asked. "He never belonged in the city," he replied. "In the village, he would have been a powerful man; he was clever, and knew how to talk to people. But no one lives in the villages now; that way of life is gone." This characterization points to a further tension in Nikos's life that I have not yet touched on here. As the oldest of three brothers, Nikos normally would have been expected to take the leadership role in their common endeavors, yet he was continually told what to do by his brothers, particularly Bobbis. Nikos, they claimed, was unaware and unskilled in the necessary business skills that the complex situation in Chania's old town required. The difference in their backgammon styles, then, reflected for Bobbis (and others who shared his view about Nikos) Nikos's inability to navigate the complex and often shifting tourist business in the city. This business is marked by deep uncertainties from year to year because of regional crises that may vastly reduce the number of tourists in the country each summer. In addition, frequent changes in the tax laws during the period in which I was in Chania (1994 until early 1996) led one business owner to argue that the greatest risk owners faced was these changes, not the possibility of few tourists (see chapter 4). Further complications, such as managing one's affairs with the local historical conservation office, added to the task (see Herzfeld 1991). Nikos was marginalized in the decision making by his two brothers and often had little to do during the long afternoons at the hotel, and this lack of responsibility lent further weight to the comments by others that characterized him as from the wrong era.

This accounting for Nikos's death by reference to his achronicity, if you will, is importantly similar to what Fabian calls the "denial of coevalness." Fabian (1983, 31) defines it as "a persistent and systematic tendency to place the referent(s) of anthropology in a Time other that the present of the producer of anthropological discourse." Obviously the case of Nikos and his achronicity is not a systematic or persistent one, however; it is instead an ad hoc account of his death by placing him out of time. What is more, this case is not about the denial of coevalness as practiced by a discipline (or the West generally) against the people who are the subject of study. Instead, and crucially, this example opens our eyes to the possibility of the deployment of ideas about time, contingency, and stances toward the future *within* a particular context. In this vein, a Chaniot might characterize Bobbis's style of playing backgam-

mon as contemporary, of this time, and as therefore reflecting a current
and rational approach to chance. That of Nikos, by contrast, an approach
guided more by his interest in social performance than by a narrow pursuit of victory, lies, according to this view, in a fatalist past. Such strategic representations are a key element of the politics of contingency. In
this respect, inability or unwillingness to perform the normatively rec-
ommended means to approach chance (statistical probability) reflects a
shortcoming in the cosmologic domain as well. If one does not deploy
the expected trope of chance, risk, then one must, the logic goes, be fatalistic.

Those who did not know Nikos were even less charitable, perhaps,
than his acquaintances. Whereas the placing of Nikos in another time at
least portrayed his way of confronting the unexpected as valid in its own
context yet simply out of place (time), others with whom I spoke saw
Nikos's actions as those of a self-absorbed would-be *mangas* (pl., *manges*).
The image of the *mangas* is a common one in Greece. It refers to the dramatic, self-sufficient, antiestablishment figure associated with the musical subculture of *rebetiko* in 1920s urban Greece (see Cowan 1990, 173–75,
for a concise account of this figure). *Manges* danced *zeibekiko* well, walked
with a characteristic swagger, wore their fedoras low on their brows,
smoked marijuana, and gambled with flair. To connect Nikos to this image
in a disparaging way is another technique for placing him out of time, yet
it links him to a figure that was always largely marginal to Greek society,
and although the image has its positive connotations, particularly among
the gamblers of Chania, it is on the whole an idea of Greek manhood that
many Chaniots find embarrassingly "un-European." In this account, then,
Nikos first failed to perform convincingly the role of the *mangas* (perhaps
because of both inappropriate context and inability) and is further suspect
because he aspired to be an "un-European" Greek in the first place. Again,
as in the previous discussion, the attitude toward chance is a key element
in the distancing of Nikos's actions from those of other Chaniots and, by
extension, thus accounting for his death.

However, this issue reminds us that Nikos's own approach to the
contingent was not so idiosyncratic as to be nonsensical to other Chaniots. The instances of his successful social performance (both on my
nameday and while dancing at the club) show that his approach to chance
was itself embedded in a larger, socially coherent set of ways to confront
chance. Thus, to some other Chaniots, he was not inscrutable but rather
was putting forth an approach to the contingent that failed on more
specific grounds (out of place, out of time). And other Chaniots did not
speak so dismissively of Nikos and his way of life. One close friend said

simply that he will miss Nikos and always respect him. I was unable to press this contact further on this sensitive point, yet it suggests that for this friend Nikos's integrity to his own way of being was worthy of lasting admiration.

Nikos's family varied somewhat in their attempts to account for his death. In fact, his brothers and his widow were marked by a silence on the matter, even among themselves, a stance that reminds us of the ultimately personal, affective, and ineffable features of such engagements of chance. Nikos's mother explicitly rejected this silence on the issue, however. During the evening that I joined her, Nikos's widow, and their two daughters for dinner, Nikos's mother repeatedly and somewhat uncomfortably asked her daughter-in-law and grandchildren, "Why? Why do we not talk about him? We must remember him and enjoy his memory." His widow and the older daughter only nodded silently, the younger daughter fled the room, crying, upon the second or third such statement. Yet Nikos's mother did not relent: "He was a good son, a good man." Indeed, the parallel between her willingness to charge forward into potentially distressing social situations and Nikos's similar quality struck me strongly in the midst of the evening and brought my own sense of loss close to the surface. As I said my goodbye at the end of a long evening, Nikos's mother joined me as I left. Giving me a traditional and colorful handwoven bag made by a relative who still lived in their village in Sfakia, she told me that I was a good friend to Nikos, and not to forget her son. She turned away abruptly and strode purposefully back to her home.

A Chance Ending

Examining Nikos's personal attitude toward risk provides the startling realization that even the confrontation of our own ultimate ends, our mortality, may be an arena for constituting selfhood and that this process may often take precedence over a narrow evaluation of risk in a utilitarian sense. As Sandra Gifford (1986) reminds us, such statistical reasoning about chance provides very little in the way of meaning or even prediction in discrete instances. What is more, Nikos's story attests to the usefulness of an approach that sees how someone may bring into juxtaposition different domains of indeterminacy as a part of this constitution of self. In this case, a person's demonstrated ability to confront chance in one arena attests to that person's ability in other domains.

At the broader social level, events such as Nikos's death can become, because of their very lack of ultimate resolution, fodder for either individuals' or institutions' attempts to establish legitimacy. Admittedly,

Nikos's death, which because of my close relationship with him provides a wealth of material on the side of individual engagements of chance, did not become a prominent focus of such struggles. In fact, it is the very taken-for-granted quality of the event itself that illuminates the social processes at work. One of countless such events that in official discourse are interpreted and left behind, Nikos's death pointedly did *not* come to provide grounds for any doubt about the discourse of traffic safety, for example, in Greece.

Much remains to be done in such a renovation of our ideas about the politics of contingency. Social life is rife with such examples, and yet it is the other social sciences that largely have dictated our own approaches toward understanding contingency. Economics, in particular, has long been concerned with how actors make decisions in the context of an uncertain future, but such rational choice theory approaches are founded on the same assumptions discussed earlier. Anthropology in general is in a unique position to explore personal and public engagements of chance and to approach these events without an overly normative scheme. In this way anthropology can usefully expand on insights it has already gained by exploring the uses of the past and come to understand how this contested past may be linked to an unfolding present and claims to legitimacy in the future.

I have been concerned in this work with exploring how gamblers and other Chaniots account for the unfolding of unpredictable outcomes and thereby construct a momentary reality in the context of an approaching future that is always at root uncertain. The sources of this indeterminacy can usefully be considered to fall within several domains, from the formal indeterminacy of discrete events to performative, social and cosmologic forms, although these domains often are simultaneously present over the gaming table. I have furthermore argued that a key aspect of this engagement of chance involves positioning oneself or others within an emergent understanding of the present and that these claims are made performatively. Thus, a (dis)ordering of reality takes place in gaming contexts, one that arises between the participants (and other spectators) rather than solely within each actor's experience. Gambling, though a part of everyday experience with significant consequences, nonetheless provides a semibounded refraction of the precarious nature of everyday experience, a kind of distillation of a chanceful life into a seemingly more apprehensible form.

Chaniots make these connections themselves and further connect ideas about risk, uncertainty, and gambling to local claims about class, the social and historical landscape, and broader concerns about European-

ness. What is at stake in the contests, over gaming tables, business transactions, political maneuverings, and gender relations, is one's own always
tenuous position vis-à-vis the unfolding present and future to come. In
this sense, gambling in Chania is gambling one's life, as Nikos's story con-
veys most poignantly.

Notes

1. I have also used the story of Nikos to interrogate the concept of risk in medical anthropology (Malaby 2002). Many of the same details are also presented here,
but the story is put to use for the different and broader analytical purpose of this
book.

2. Bound up in this action on Nikos's part, and in that of other men in Chania
who adopt a style of instrumental nonchalance, are issues of manhood similar
to those Herzfeld (1985) has examined, but he has also described a similar kind
of action, a defiance of destiny, in the context of a Cretan funeral, where again
the stakes were mortal but where, interestingly, the actor was a woman (Herzfeld
1993).

3. This quote may also be a reference to the leaders of the *junta*, the military
group that held power in Greece from 1967 to 1974, who are currently in jail, a
group one Chaniot called *i filakismeni* ("the imprisoned").

APPENDIX

Here I list the various card games I encountered in Chania, both those regularly played and others described or demonstrated to me, and explain the rules for those I came to know well. Some of these card games vary little or not at all from corresponding games as described in the standard reference on games in the United States, *Hoyle's Rules of Games* (Morehead and Mott-Smith 1983; hereafter *Hoyle's*), and I have noted this in each such entry. I have also grouped similar card games together and noted established variations. (I describe *zaria*, or dice gambling, in the main text. A thorough description of the forms of backgammon played in Chania [*portes, fevga,* and *plakoto*] would include extensive diagrams and is beyond the technical scope of this work.)

Koum-Kan: Very similar to the game rummy, this game has a name very close to one that *Hoyle's* describes as "the ancestor of all rummy games," Coon-Can (64). However, the rules of *koum-kan* more closely match continental rummy as described in *Hoyle's* (68–69). In all rummy-type games the object is to make sets of at least three of a kind (no duplicate suits) or straights of the same suit. In *koum-kan* and similar games in Chania, two decks are used (including jokers), each player is dealt ten cards, and play proceeds around the table, with each player drawing from the top of either the stack of unplayed cards (turned down) or the stack of discards and then either discarding it or exchanging it for one card in hand. As one makes the groups of three (melds) one can lay them down, although this gives the other player the opportunity to play his own individual cards on your sets and even exchange appropriate cards for wild cards in these sets. A player wins upon successfully putting all of the ten cards in melds and, in *Hoyle's* terms, "going out." All the cards not laid down when one player goes out are counted against the holding player. In *koum-kan* jokers and red aces are wild cards. Because skill is involved in the play of the hands to a significant degree, *koum-kan* is a legal game and can be played in establishments with card-playing licenses (many *kafenia*).

Thanasis: This game is a variant on *koum-kan.* As in *koum-kan*, the jokers are included and are wild, but instead of red aces, in *thanasis* all of the twos (eight cards) are wild, and the first card turned over after dealing is also wild (thus, if a five, for example, is turned over, the remaining seven fives in the deck are wild). This means that instead of six wild cards, as in *koum-kan*, there are nineteen wild cards in *thanasis*. The profusion of wild cards means the game moves very quickly; sometimes a player can go out immediately after the deal. The point value for each card is the face value of the card, with aces worth 1 point and face cards worth 10. *Thanasis*, often played for significant stakes, and involving a higher degree of chance, is illegal to play in Chania. Each player whose score reaches 101 is out of the game and owes the amount bet (equal from each player), but each such player has the option of erasing the previous hand's points and staying in by doubling the bet. Some informants categorized this game as *dhinamitis* ("dynamite"), saying that it is only one form of *thanasis*, which normally has only the jokers and turned-over card as wild (a total of eleven wild cards).

Berimba: My information on this complicated game is limited, but it appears to be similar to canasta (*Hoyle's*, 78–87).

Prefa: This is a complicated game with separate rounds for bidding and the play of the hand, as in bridge. It is also a very difficult game to score, and only a couple of my informants understood how to keep score in the game. I never learned this game well enough to describe its rules fully. *Prefa* is played with only thirty-two cards, without the two through six of each suit. Each player gets ten cards, and two cards are laid aside. Later, the player who ends the bidding (names the final contract) can exchange two of his cards for these cards after looking at them. Simpler forms of this game are *bilota* and *eksinta-eksi* (66).

Bilota: Similar to *prefa*, *bilota* is played with the seven through ace of each suit and has two parts, the bidding and trick play. Each player first receives six cards. The next card from the deck is then turned over and placed under the deck. The player who did not deal has the first chance to call the suit of the turned-over card as trump. If he passes, then the dealer has a chance. For nontrump suits, the ranking of cards (descending) is ace, ten, king, queen, jack, nine, eight, seven. For the trump suit alone, the jack and then nine are the most powerful for trick play, with the remaining cards following in the aforementioned order. If both players pass on the turned-over card, then the nondealer has the chance to name another suit. If he again passes, the dealer has a chance. If both pass, the cards are thrown in and redealt. Once the trump suit is determined, three more cards are dealt to each player and another card is turned over.

Trick play proceeds, with the declarer beginning. The goal is to accumulate points, primarily through winning tricks. Only aces through jacks have value: aces, 11; tens, 10; kings, 4; queens, 3; and jacks, 2. One also gets 10 points for taking the final trick, 20 points for king-queen in trump ("*bilota*"), 20 points for any series of three cards of one suit (as long as the opposing player does not have a higher series, which cancels the lower; equal series cancel each other), and 20 points for each further card of a straight in a suit. Finally, having all four of one kind of card is worth very high bonus points, with four tens, queens, kings, and aces worth 100 points each, four nines worth 150, and four jacks worth 200. The game is often played until one player reaches 777 points, but sometimes it is only to 555 or 666.

Eksinta-Eksi (66): This game, similar to *bilota*, is played with only twenty-four cards, the nine through the ace of each suit. It is a simpler game than *prefa*. As in *bilota*, the ten is more powerful than all other cards except the ace. For two players, each is dealt six cards. The next card is turned over and placed under the deck. The suit of this card becomes trump automatically. Play proceeds in tricks. After each trick each player draws another card from the deck, the previous trick's winner first. As one collects cards one gets points for each of them as follows: ace, 11; ten, 10; king, 4; queen, 3; jack, 2; and nine, 0. As in *bilota*, if a player has the king and queen in any suit but trump and shows it before playing one of them, he gets 20 points automatically. If the pair is in trump, he gets 40 points. In addition, the player with the nine of trump can trade it, after winning a trick, for the trump card turned over and placed under the deck after the deal. The first player to 66 points wins. If the losing player has no points after any given hand, the loss is tripled. If he has less than 33 points but more than zero, the loss is doubled. There are further subtleties. For example, either player can declare the deck "closed" at any time and play out the hands as they are.

Skabili ("Slap"): Very similar to *eksinta-eksi*, this game involves trick play and a determined trump suit. In this form, however, a full deck is used, and the three, not the ten, is the second most powerful card in all suits. The two teams of six players try to communicate in gestures what trump cards they have according to strict conventions, thus hoping to prompt their partners into leading the right suits or otherwise making correct plays. The gesture for each trump card is as follows:

Ace	Winking
3	Twitching one side of one's mouth back
K	Nodding
Q	Shrugging one shoulder
J	Pursing one's lips out, as if scratching an itch on the underside of one's nose with one's mustache (fittingly, this gesture is called *to moustakhio*).

The remaining cards are signified by rubbing the tips of one's fingers together.

Poker: As described in the text, this game is in many respects identical to draw poker as described in *Hoyle's* (41–43), except that it is for four players (sometimes three), and only the seven through ace of each suit are used (for three players, the eight through ace of each suit are used).

Poka: This game is very similar to stud poker as described in *Hoyle's* (44–45). I never observed *poka* played in Chania, but it was mentioned on numerous occasions.

Ikosi-Ena (21): This game is identical to blackjack as described in *Hoyle's* (180–83). I observed it only around the New Year.

Treanta-Ena (31): This game is very similar to thirty-one as described in *Hoyle's* (183–84). It is a variation on blackjack, except that the object is to get as close as possible to 31 points in one's cards without going over. Having 14 points in one's cards also wins, however, and players win immediately upon reaching 14 or 31 points.

Koupes: This game is identical to the game of hearts as described in *Hoyle's* (118–19).

Britz: This game is in all respects identical to contract bridge as described in *Hoyle's* (1–26). As in the United States, there is some variation in conventions between the players, and all agree before each contest on which will be used by each team.

Khorai Dhen Khorai: This game is played with one deck, and each player is dealt two cards and bets on whether the value of the next dealt card will be in between his cards.

REFERENCES CITED

Anand, Paul. 1993. *Foundations of Rational Choice under Risk*. Oxford, U.K.: Clarendon Press.

Asad, Talal. 1993. *Genealogies of Religion: Discipline and Reasons of Power in Christianity and Islam*. Baltimore: Johns Hopkins University Press.

Austin, J. L. 1975 [1956]. *How to Do Things with Words*. Cambridge, Mass.: Harvard University Press.

Bauman, Richard. 1977. *Verbal Art as Performance*. Prospect Heights, Ill.: Waveland Press.

Beauvoir, Simone de. 1952. *The Second Sex*. Trans. and ed. H. M. Parshley. New York: Knopf.

Beck, Ulrich. 1992. *Risk Society: Towards a New Modernity*. London: Sage.

Becker, Gay. 1997. *Disrupted Lives: How People Create Meaning in a Chaotic World*. Berkeley: University of California Press.

Borneman, John. 1992. *Belonging in the Two Berlins: Kin, State, and Nation*. Cambridge, U.K.: Cambridge University Press.

Bosk, Charles L. 1979. *Forgive and Remember: Managing Medical Failure*. Chicago: University of Chicago Press.

Bourdieu, Pierre. 1977. *Outline of a Theory of Practice*. Cambridge, U.K.: Cambridge University Press.

———. 1989. "Social Space and Symbolic Power." *Sociological Theory* 7 (1): 14–25.

Campbell, J. K. 1964. *Honour, Family, and Patronage: A Study of Institutions and Moral Values in a Greek Mountain Community*. Oxford, U.K.: Oxford University Press.

Carrier, James. 1992. "Occidentalism: The World Turned Upside-Down." *American Ethnologist* 19 (2): 195–212.

Chapple, Richard. 1983. *A Dostoevsky Dictionary*. Ann Arbor, Mich.: Ardis.

Coulson, Jessie. 1966. "Introduction." In *The Gambler. Bobok. A Nasty Story.* 7–16. New York: Penguin Books.

Cowan, Jane. 1990. *Dance and the Body Politic in Northern Greece*. Princeton, N.J.: Princeton University Press.

Crapanzano, Vincent. 1986. "Hermes' Dilemma: The Masking of Subversion in Ethnographic Description." In *Writing Culture: The Poetics and Politics of Ethnography*. Ed. James Clifford and George Marcus. 51–76. Berkeley: University of California Press.

Csordas, Thomas J. 1993. "Somatic Modes of Attention." *Cultural Anthropology* 8 (2): 135–56.

Damer, Seán. 1988. "Legless in Sfakiá: Drinking and Social Practice in Western Crete." *Journal of Modern Greek Studies* 6: 291–310.

Delakis, Mikhalis. 1995. "Ton Prosilkien exeretika i prasini trapeza." *Kirix*, December 20, p. 13.

Detorakis, Theocharis E. 1994. *History of Crete*. Trans. John C. Davis. Iraklion, Crete: T. Detorakis.

Dostoevsky, Fyodor. 1972 [1866]. *The Gambler, with Polina Suslova's Diary*. Ed. Edward Wasiolek. Trans. Victor Terras. Chicago: University of Chicago Press.

Douglas, Mary. 1966. *Purity and Danger: An Analysis of Concepts of Pollution and Taboo*. New York: Praeger.

———. 1992. *Risk and Blame: Essays in Cultural Theory*. London: Routledge.

Douglas, Mary, and Baron Isherwood. 1978. *The World of Goods: Towards an Anthropology of Consumption*. Harmondsworth, U.K.: Penguin Books.

du Boulay, Juliet. 1974. *Portrait of a Greek Mountain Village*. Oxford, U.K.: Clarendon Press.

Dubisch, Jill, ed. 1986. *Gender and Power in Rural Greece*. Princeton, N.J.: Princeton University Press.

Fabian, Johannes. 1983. *Time and the Other: How Anthropology Makes Its Object*. New York: Columbia University Press.

Falk, Pasi, and Pasi Mäenpää. 1999. *Hitting the Jackpot: Lives of Lottery Millionaires*. Oxford, U.K.: Berg.

Faubion, James D. 1993. *Modern Greek Lessons: A Primer in Historical Constructivism*. Princeton, N.J.: Princeton University Press.

Ferguson, James. 1990. *The Anti-Politics Machine: "Development," Depoliticization, and Bureaucratic Power in Lesotho*. Cambridge, U.K.: Cambridge University Press.

Fernandez, James. 1986. *Persuasions and Performances: The Play of Tropes in Culture*. Bloomington: Indiana University Press.

Frankenberg, Ronald. 1993. "Risk: Anthropological and Epidemiological Narratives of Prevention." In *Knowledge, Power, and Practice: The Anthropology of Medicine and Everyday Life*. Ed. Shirley Lindenbaum and Margaret Lock. 219–42. Berkeley: University of California Press.

Friedrich, Paul. 1986. *The Language Parallax*. Austin: University of Texas Press.

Gardiner, Michael. 1992. *The Dialogics of Critique: M. M. Bakhtin and the Theory of Ideology*. London: Routledge.

Geertz, Clifford. 1973. *The Interpretation of Cultures*. New York: Basic Books.

Giddens, Anthony. 1984. *The Constitution of Society: Outline of the Theory of Structuration*. Berkeley: University of California Press.

———. 1991. *Modernity and Self-Identity: Self and Society in the Late Modern Age*. Stanford, Calif.: Stanford University Press.

Gifford, Sandra M. 1986. "The Meaning of Lumps: A Case Study of the Ambiguities of Risk." In *Anthropology and Epidemiology*. Ed. Craig Janes, Ron Stall, and Sandra Gifford. 213–46. Dordrecht, Netherlands: D. Reidel.

Godelier, Maurice. 1972. *Rationality and Irrationality in Economics*. Trans. Brian Pearce. New York: Monthly Review Press.

Good, Byron. 1994. *Medicine, Rationality, and Experience: An Anthropological Perspective*. Cambridge, U.K.: Cambridge University Press.

Green, Donald P., and Ian Shapiro. 1994. *Pathologies of Rational Choice Theory: A Critique of Applications in Political Science*. New Haven, Conn.: Yale University Press.

Guterson, David. 1995. *Snow Falling on Cedars*. New York: Vintage Books.

Hacking, Ian. 1975. *The Emergence of Probability*. Cambridge, U.K.: Cambridge University Press.

———. 1990. *The Taming of Chance*. Cambridge, U.K.: Cambridge University Press.

Hamilakis, Yannis, and Eleana Yalouri. 1999. "Sacralising the Past: The Cults of Archaeology in Modern Greece." *Archaeological Dialogues* 6 (2): 115–60.

Hart, Laurie Kain. 1992. *Time, Religion, and Social Experience in Rural Greece*. Lanham, Md.: Rowman and Littlefield.

Herzfeld, Michael. 1981. "Meaning and Morality: A Semiotic Approach to Evil Eye Accusations in a Greek Village." *American Ethnologist* 8 (3): 560–74.

———. 1985. *Poetics of Manhood: Contest and Identity in a Cretan Mountain Village*. Princeton, N.J.: Princeton University Press.

———. 1987. *Anthropology through the Looking-Glass: Critical Ethnography in the Margins of Europe*. Cambridge, U.K.: Cambridge University Press.

———. 1991. *A Place in History: Social and Monumental Time in a Cretan Town*. Princeton, N.J.: Princeton University Press.

———. 1992. *The Social Production of Indifference: Exploring the Roots of Western Bureaucracy*. London: Berg.

———. 1993. "In Defiance of Destiny: The Management of Time and Gender at a Cretan Funeral." *American Ethnologist* 20 (2): 241–55.

———. 1997a. *Cultural Intimacy: Social Poetics in the Nation-State*. New York: Routledge.

———. 1997b. *Portrait of a Greek Imagination: An Ethnographic Biography of Andreas Nenedakis*. Chicago: University of Chicago Press.

Heyman, Josiah M., ed. 1999. *States and Illegal Practices*. Oxford, U.K.: Berg.

Hirschon, Reneé. 1981. "Essential Objects and the Sacred: Interior and Exterior Space in an Urban Greek Locality." In *Women and Space: Ground Rules and Social Maps*. Ed. Shirley Ardener. 72–88. New York: St. Martin's Press.

Hood, Christopher. 1996. "Control over Bureaucracy: Cultural Theory and Institutional Variety." *Journal of Public Policy* 15 (3): 207–30.

———. 1998. *The Art of the State: Culture, Rhetoric, and Public Management*. Oxford, U.K.: Clarendon Press.

Horn, Kevin. 1996. "Greece Pulls in the Punters." *Financial Times*, November 12, p. 27.

Jackson, Michael. 1989. *Paths toward a Clearing: Radical Empiricism and Ethnographic Inquiry*. Bloomington: Indiana University Press.

Jenkins, Timothy. 1994. "Fieldwork and the Perception of Everyday Life." *Man* (n.s.) 29 (2): 433–55.

Karp, Ivan. 1986. "Agency and Social Theory: A Review of Anthony Giddens." *American Ethnologist* 13 (1): 131–37.

Kaufert, Patricia A., and John O'Neil. 1993. "Analysis of a Dialogue on Risks in Childbirth." In *Knowledge, Power, and Practice: The Anthropology of Medicine and Everyday Life*. Ed. Shirley Lindenbaum and Margaret Lock. 32–54. Berkeley: University of California Press.

Keane, Webb. 1997. *Signs of Recognition: Powers and Hazards of Representation in an Indonesian Society*. Berkeley: University of California Press.

Kleinman, Arthur, and Joan Kleinman. 1991. "Suffering and Its Professional Transformation: Toward an Ethnography of Interpersonal Experience." *Culture, Medicine, and Psychiatry* 15 (3): 275–301.

Lichtenstein, Sarah, and Paul Slovic. 1971. "Response-Induced Reversals of Preference in Gambling: An Extended Replication in Las Vegas." *Journal of Experimental Psychology* 101: 16–20.

Loizos, Peter, and Evthymios Papataxiarchis, eds. 1991. *Contested Identities: Gender and Kinship in Modern Greece.* Princeton, N.J.: Princeton University Press.

MacIntyre, Alasdair. 1984. *After Virtue: A Study in Moral Theory.* 2d ed. Notre Dame, Ind.: University of Notre Dame Press.

Malaby, Thomas M. 1999. "Fateful Misconceptions: Rethinking Paradigms of Chance among Gamblers in Crete." *Social Analysis* 43 (1): 141–65.

———. 2002. "Odds and Ends: Risk, Mortality, and the Politics of Contingency." *Culture, Medicine, and Psychiatry* 26 (3): 283–312.

———. In press. "Spaces in Tense: History, Contingency, and Place in a Cretan City." In *The Usable Past: Greek Metahistories.* Ed. Keith Brown and Yannis Hamilakis. Ranham, Md.: Rowman and Littlefield.

Maltezopoulou, Antonis B. 1982. *To Tavli: Omorfia kai Axia.* Athens: n.p.

Mann, Thomas. 1945. "Introduction." In *The Short Novels of Dostoevsky.* vii–xx. New York: Dial Press.

Mauss, Marcel. 1990 [1925]. *The Gift.* New York: W.W. Norton and Co.

March, James G., and Johan P. Olsen. 1989. *Rediscovering Institutions: The Organizational Basis of Politics.* New York: Free Press.

Moore, Sally Falk. 1978. *Law as Process: An Anthropological Approach.* London: Routledge and Kegan Paul.

———. 1987. "Explaining the Present: Theoretical Dilemmas in Processual Ethnography." *American Ethnologist* 14 (4): 727–36.

Morehead, Albert H., and Geoffrey Mott-Smith, eds. 1983. *Hoyle's Rules of Games.* 2d. rev. ed. New York: Penguin Books.

Nicholson, Walter. 1985. *Microeconomic Theory: Basic Principles and Extensions.* 3d ed. New York: Dryden Press.

Oxfeld, Ellen. 1993. *Blood, Sweat, and Mahjong: Family and Enterprise in an Overseas Chinese Community.* Ithaca, N.Y.: Cornell University Press.

Papataxiarchis, Evthymios. 1991. "Friends of the Heart: Male Commensal Solidarity, Gender, and Kinship in Aegean Greece." In *Contested Identities: Gender and Kinship in Modern Greece.* Ed. Peter Loizos and Evthymios Papataxiarchis. 156–79. Princeton, N.J.: Princeton University Press.

Roseberry, William. 1982. "Balinese Cockfights and the Seduction of Anthropology." *Social Research* 49 (4): 1013–28.

Rosenthal, Franz. 1975. *Gambling in Islam.* Leiden, Netherlands: E. J. Brill.

Sutton, David. 1997. "Local Names, Foreign Claims: Family Inheritance and National Heritage on a Greek Island." *American Ethnologist* 24 (2): 415–37.

Tambiah, Stanley Jeyarajah. 1990. *Magic, Science, Religion, and the Scope of Rationality.* New York: Cambridge University Press.

Tsivis, Yiannis. 1993. *Chania, 1252–1940.* Athens, Greece: Gnosis Publishers.

Urla, Jacqueline. 1993. "Cultural Politics in an Age of Statistics: Numbers, Nations, and the Making of Basque Identity." *American Ethnologist* 20 (4): 818–43.

Wasiolek, Edward. 1972. "Introduction." In *The Gambler, with Polina Suslova's Diary.* vii–xxxix. Chicago: University of Chicago Press.

Weber, Max. 1930. *The Protestant Ethic and Spirit of Capitalism.* Trans. Talcott Parsons. London: Harper Collins Academic.

———. 1946. *From Max Weber: Essays in Sociology.* Ed. and Trans. H. H. Gerth and C. Wright Mills. New York: Oxford University Press.

Whyte, Susan Reynolds. 1997. *Questioning Misfortune: The Pragmatics of Uncertainty in Eastern Uganda.* Cambridge, U.K.: Cambridge University Press.

Wilson, Bryan, ed. 1970. *Rationality.* Oxford, U.K.: Basil Blackwell.

Zimmer, Laura. 1986. "Card Playing among the Gende: A System for Keeping Money and Social Relationships Alive." *Oceania* 56 (4): 245–63.

———. 1987. "Gambling with Cards in Melanesia and Australia." *Oceania* 58 (1): 1–59.

INDEX

THOMAS M. MALABY is an assistant professor of anthropology at the University of Wisconsin at Milwaukee. He has published articles in *Social Analysis, Anthropological Quarterly, Culture, Medicine, and Psychiatry,* and the *Journal of the Society for the Anthropology of Europe.*

The University of Illinois Press
is a founding member of the
Association of American University Presses.

Composed in 9.5/12.5 Trump Mediaeval
with Trump Mediaeval display
by Type One, LLC
for the University of Illinois Press
Manufactured by Thomson-Shore, Inc.

University of Illinois Press
1325 South Oak Street
Champaign, IL 61820-6903
www.press.uillinois.edu